Martin Yan
The Chinese Chef

By
Martin Yan

YAN CAN COOK

Managing Editor
LINDA BRANDT

Art Director
RON HARPER

Photographer
NIKOLAY ZUREK

Editor
MARIE KRATSIOS

Text Researchers & Contributors
JANET IKEDA
RICHARD KANES
LINDA MEAD
JAN NIX

Illustrator
PAULINE PHUNG

Cover Designer
BRUCE MARION

Calligrapher
CHUNG-KWONG CHEUNG

Typesetter
FRANK'S TYPE

Printer
BRIGHT FUTURE PRINTING CO., LTD.

Printing Coordinator
DRAGON SEEDS CO., LTD.

Props for Photography
CECILIA CHIANG, MANDARIN RESTAURANT
CANTON BAZAAR

Published simultaneously by Doubleday Canada Limited,
Toronto, Canada.

Library of Congress Cataloging-in-Publication Data:
Yan, Martin   **Martin Yan — the Chinese Chef.**
1. Cookery, Chinese .   I. Title.   II. Title: Chinese Chef.
TX724.5.C5Y283   1985   641.5951 Library of Congress Catalog
Card Number 85-20631

ISBN 0-385-23412-0

Sixth Printing July, 1999

Every book starts with an idea from one person, but flourishes with the help and hard work of others. Without this group of talented friends and associates, this book might not have been ready in time for the new television show and for you. And, then you might have said that Yan Can Cook, but "Where's the book?"

Linda Brandt's drive and creative force as coordinator and food stylist on this entire project has brought me a new appreciation of the art form. And, my heartfelt thanks to Nikolay Zurek, the talented and very patient photographer of this book; and to Ron Harper, whose special design talents you see here.

To Linda Mead, who took the bull by the horn coordinating the information in this book, I owe a special thanks. And, to Jan Nix, an expert on Oriental foods and a dear friend, who kept the direction of this project in perspective. Many thanks to Richard Kanes for his tireless efforts in researching, writing, and editing. For her helpful and artful illustrations, Pauline Phung.

For their many hours of slaving over a hot wok while testing the recipes in this book, thanks to Janet Ikeda and Donna Garbesi. And, Melinda Larson, our wizard at the computer; Cathy Chan, for her expert Chinese translations. To Howard Fisher, my adopted brother, "See, I really can cook!"

Without Irene Chriss, director of our new cooking school, Menus, everything would literally have collapsed around our ears. Irene worked diligently to open the school while we had our noses in the book. And, I cannot forget my friends, Rocky and Irma Kalish, who taught me to laugh and see the humor in life.

At Doubleday, many thanks to the talented executive editor, Les Pockel; to Maria Kratsios, my personal editor; and to Tom Murray, who has believed in me and been most helpful since my first book.

And, I wouldn't be telling you about the joy of wokking without Margie Poore of KQED-TV, wok-aholic and executive producer of "Yan Can Cook." She helped make the show a hit.

But, most of all, I cannot forget the one person that is always there for me, sharing my vision. My wife, Sue. Her undaunted patience, even temperament, and support kept me going through the long, arduous hours. And, her gentle nudges got me up in the mornings to start again. And, my Mom in China and brother Michael in Toronto, who eagerly await my new book.

To you, and to all my friends and viewers, I dedicate this book. Many thanks.

THANKS

TABLE OF CONTENTS

China has had its share of droughts and food shortages through the ages. This scarcity has made the preparing and eating of food a preoccupation which is reflected in the diversity of the cuisine. As early as the Han dynasty (206 B.C.–A.D. 220), the five flavors—sweet, sour, salty, bitter, and hot—were experimented with, blended, defined, and incorporated into numerous taste combinations.

The cooking of China has been shaped by the geography of China, which contains a multitude of climates and resources. Chinese cuisine is the product of five thousand years of many regional cultures blending to form a fascinating culinary experience.

The best way to grasp the diversity of China's cuisine is to consider the land as divided into four major culinary regions, each boasting its own cultural identity. Regional cooking styles have thrived in their respective locales throughout China's long and complex history: from the bustling seaports of the eastern coast to the landlocked, humid central provinces, from the dry northeastern plains to the lush, subtropical south.

Over the years, certain regional dishes have become popular outside their native provinces. Chinese cuisine is highly innovative, and chefs constantly try new dishes with new ingredients. Oftentimes, some of the best Chinese food is found in large, cosmopolitan cities, such as Guangzhou (Canton), Shanghai, or Beijing (Peking).

This book accompanies my sixth television season of "Yan Can Cook" and is organized by culinary regions with a special section on innovative Nouvelle Chinese dishes. The selection of recipes is diverse; some are familiar, and some are more exotic. Besides the recipes demonstrated on the cooking show, I have included many more popular dishes in the book. (For purposes of variety, a few dishes may have

Martin Yan, the Chinese Chef

been placed out of their areas of origin.) You'll also find that this book is packed with informative pointers on technique. Once you master the basic techniques, all you need is imagination. Remember, the cookbook only serves as a guide.

As I began to compile the recipes for this book, I stopped to reflect on just how far I've come in my career. When I was young, my father ran a small family restaurant. Literally, I got in the food business on the ground floor. As a little kid, I spent most of my time crawling around under the tables. That's how I developed a taste for food. My mom opened a grocery store after my father passed away, so I was exposed to a variety of foods. Soon after, I left China; this was back in 1963. I travelled to Hong Kong where, to my chagrin, my uncle put me to work in his restaurant. One of the head cooks at the restaurant loved horse racing and spent most of his time at the tracks so he never had much time to cook. Needless to say, my first memories of Hong Kong looked like the inside of a wok. As I sliced, chopped, and generally fried away in my uncle's restaurant, I never dreamed that I would one day be on national television in North America.

Through the 560 television shows I've hosted since 1978, I have enjoyed sharing many delicious recipes with you. It is a good feeling to reach people and to make them smile while doing something that I enjoy. This cookbook is my latest gift to you, my friends and audience. I thank you for supporting the "Yan Can Cook" show, and I wish you a good life and many years of happy dining.

Martin Yan, the Chinese Chef

Martin Yan, the Chinese Chef

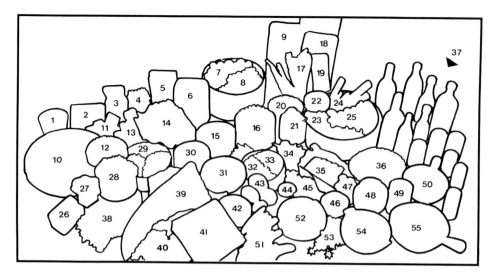

Key for pages 8 and 9

1) glutinous rice 2) water chestnut powder 3) bean thread noodles 4) dried flat egg noodles 5) glutinous rice powder 6) rice stick noodles 7) dried lychees 8) dried red dates 9) dried bean curd 10) long-grain rice 11) dried rice crusts 12) skinned dried mung beans 13) dried egg noodles 14) dried rice noodles 15) gingko nuts 16) peanuts 17) dried bean curd sticks 18) dried bean curd sheets 19) spiced pressed bean curd 20) cloud ears 21) fermented black beans 22) tiger lily buds 23) wood ears 24) Chinese cinnamon sticks 25) dried black mushrooms 26) Oolong tea 27) jasmine tea 28) Chinese black tea 29) mung beans, red beans, soy beans 30) peanuts, skins removed 31) cashew nuts 32) white sesame seeds 33) black sesame seeds 34) dried tangerine peel 35) Chinese brown sugar 36) Chinese seaweed 37) Chinese sauces & condiments 38) Chinese bo-li black tea 39) dried shark's fin 40) snow mushrooms 41) dried bird's nest 42) dried lotus seeds 43) preserved duck eggs 44) crushed red chili peppers 45) cardamom seeds 46) Szechuan peppercorns 47) crystallized ginger 48) red fermented bean curd 49) sweet red bean paste 50) white fermented bean curd 51) Chinese pork & duck liver sausages 52) dried shrimp 53) star anise 54) Chinese salted plums 55) Szechuan preserved vegetables

GLOSSARY

BAMBOO SHOOTS
Three crops of edible shoots from bamboo plants are harvested annually in China. Canned summer and winter varieties, packed whole or sliced, are available in North America. Store unused bamboo shoots in a covered container; refrigerate, changing water daily, for up to 1 week.

BEAN CURD
Also known as "tofu." Types include: dried (in sheets or sticks); fermented (either red or white and fermented in rice wine); fresh (in cakes or blocks); and fried (in small pouches or cubes). See also page 79.

BEAN PASTE, SWEET
Sweetened fermented soy bean paste used as a seasoning in many Szechuan and Hunan dishes.

BEAN PASTE, SWEET RED
Sweet paste made from red beans. Commonly used as a filling for pastries and buns.

BEAN SAUCE, BROWN
Also referred to as yellow bean sauce. Thick sauce made from fermented soy beans.

BEAN SPROUTS
Tender sprouts from mung beans and soy beans. See also page 122.

BIRD'S NEST
Semi-translucent gelatinous substance from nests of tiny swallows from the South China Sea. Highly prized; expensive delicacy used in soups or desserts at banquets.

BITTER MELON
Also known as "foo-gwa." See also page 56.

BLACK BEANS, FERMENTED
Small, fermented black beans with pungent aroma and salty taste. Used in Cantonese-style dishes. Sold canned or bulk in plastic bags. Store unused beans in a covered jar in a cool dry place. Rinse before using.

BOK CHOY
Also known as Chinese chard. Member of the loose-leaf cabbage family. Tender inner leaves and hearts have a gentle hint of mustard flavor.

CABBAGE, NAPA
Also known as Chinese cabbage or "siew choy." Closely resembles romaine lettuce but with a sweet, delicate flavor. Produces no odor when cooked.

CHILI OIL
Used as a condiment or to "fire-up" stir-fried dishes, chili oil is a combination of oil and hot red chili peppers. See recipe page 32.

CHILI PASTE, SZECHUAN
Paste made from fermented soy beans, chili pepper, salt, and garlic. Basic seasoning in hot Hunan and Szechuan dishes.

CILANTRO
Also known as Chinese parsley or fresh coriander. Aromatic herb with a strong, zesty taste used as a garnish or to flavor soups, poultry, or other dishes.

CORN, BABY	Special miniature variety of tender corn that matures about 3 inches in length. For Chinese cooking, buy canned water-packed corn rather than pickled.
EGGS	SALTED: Duck eggs cured in brine for several months. Whites and yolks taste salty. THOUSAND-YEAR-OLD: Duck eggs preserved in a coating of salt, calcium oxide, sodium carbonate, rice hulls, and straw ashes. Considered a delicacy; often served sliced with pickled ginger at banquets.
FIVE-SPICE, CHINESE	Blend of five spices — anise seeds, cloves, fennel, cinnamon, and Szechuan peppercorns. All-purpose seasoning, commonly used in various barbecued dishes.
FUZZY MELON	Also known as hairy melon. Resembles a fat zucchini with slightly hairy skin. Used in soups and stir-fried dishes, or stuffed with meat and steamed.
GINGER	FRESH: Gnarled, tan-colored root with spicy flavor and aroma; indispensable in Chinese cooking either sliced, shredded, or grated. Choose ginger with a firm feel and lightly shiny skin. Store in a cool, dry spot. For longer storage, freeze ginger, then cut off as much as you need without thawing. Or, peel and thinly slice; store in a jar, cover with dry sherry, and refrigerate for up to 6 months. PRESERVED: Sweet, pungent condiment packed in syrup in porcelain jars, or candied and sold packaged or in bulk. PICKLED: Fresh young ginger, first pickled in salt, then preserved in vinegar and sugar.
GINGKO NUTS	Small oval-shaped nuts, sold canned or dried. Commonly used in stuffings, soups, and stews.
HAM, SMITHFIELD	Domestic ham that closely resembles delicious Yunnan ham used throughout China. Available at delicatessens and Oriental markets.
HOISIN SAUCE	Dark brown, thick sauce with a sweet, spicy flavor; made from fermented soy beans, flour, vinegar, sugar, garlic, and spices. Used to season barbecued dishes or as a dipping sauce.
HOT BEAN SAUCE	Thick sauce made from bean paste and hot chili peppers; used in most Szechuan-style dishes.
LOTUS SEEDS	Seeds of lotus flower with hard texture and delicate flavor, sold canned or dried; used in soups and sweets or like nuts for munching.
LYCHEE	Crimson, crusted tropical fruit from southern China. Meat is translucent white and sweet. Available fresh in Chinese markets during July and August; canned in light syrup; or dried to resemble raisins.

Martin Yan, the Chinese Chef

MSG	Also known as monosodium glutamate. Flavor enhancer sold under brand names, Aji-no-moto (Japanese) and Accent. Though often an ingredient in some Chinese recipes, it is not called for in this book.
MUSHROOMS	DRIED BLACK: Richly-flavored, aromatic mushroom that combines well with most ingredients. Soak in enough warm water to cover for 30 minutes before using. SNOW: Also known as white fungus. Crunchy-textured fungus used in soups and desserts. See also page 96. STRAW: Also known as grass mushrooms. Subtle flavor with a crunchy texture. Available in cans. TREE MUSHROOMS (EARS): Also known as cloud ears or wood ears. See also page 75.
MUSTARD, CHINESE	Table condiment used as a dipping sauce for meats, seafood, and savory pastries. See recipe page 32.
MUSTARD GREEN, CHINESE	Also known as "gai choy." Member of the cabbage family with a bittersweet taste; more pungent in flavor than most Chinese vegetables.
NOODLES	BEAN THREAD: Also known as cellophane noodles. Made from mung bean flour, then dried to resemble stiff nylon fishing line. Soak in warm water for 20 minutes before using in stir-fried dishes or soups, or deep-fry and use as a crunchy garnish. DRIED: Wheat flour noodles that have been dried; used in soups or stir-fried dishes. FRESH: Also known as "mein." Wheat flour noodles, often containing egg, found in various thicknesses in plastic bags. Refrigerate for up to 5 days or freeze. RICE STICK: Also known as "mai fun" or rice sticks. Made from rice flour, these noodles are more brittle than bean thread noodles.
OYSTER SAUCE	Dark brown, pungent sauce made from oyster extract, salt, and modified starch. Widely used in Cantonese cooking as a seasoning or dipping sauce. Refrigerate unused sauce for up to 3 months.
PICKLED VEGETABLES	Cucumber, carrot, turnip, and mustard green—all typical pickled vegetables with sweet and sour taste used throughout China. Available canned in Oriental markets. Store unused portions in glass jars for up to 6 months.
PLUM SAUCE	Sweet, pungent, yellow-brown sauce commonly used as a seasoning or dipping sauce. Made from salted plums, vinegar, sugar, sweet potato, chili peppers, and seasonings. Sold in bottles or cans. Transfer unused portion to an airtight jar and refrigerate for up to 6 months. See recipe page 33.

RICE	LONG-GRAIN: Staple in most southern Chinese regions. Cooks up dry and fluffy, with grains separated. Commonly used in fried rice dishes. MEDIUM-GRAIN: Available mostly in California, it closely resembles long-grain rice; has a fine flavor and aroma. SHORT-GRAIN and GLUTINOUS (SWEET): Pearly, slightly transparent in appearance; becomes soft, moist, and sticky when cooked. Used as a stuffing for duck dishes and is also commonly wrapped with other ingredients in lotus or bamboo leaves, then steamed and served as a dim sum dish.
RICE FLOUR	Finely-powdered flour made from long-grain or glutinous rice. Used in pastries and dumplings.
RICE VINEGAR	Three varieties: WHITE is used for sweet and sour dishes; RED is used as a dipping sauce; BLACK is used in braising and as a dipping sauce. All are less pungent and more flavorful than distilled white vinegar.
ROCK SUGAR	Also known as rock candy. Pale brown, less refined variety of crystallized sugar.
SAUSAGE, CHINESE	Also known as "lop cheong," these flavorful 6-inch links are made from pork, pork fat, or duck liver, and are seasoned with varying amounts of soy sauce, wine, and sugar. Steam or stir-fry to cook. May be refrigerated for up to 6 months.
SEAWEED	Also known as "nori." Delicately-flavored processed seaweed, purple in color and available dried. A common ingredient used in soups.
SESAME OIL	Concentrated, strong-flavored oil made from toasted sesame seeds. Widely used throughout China in marinades, soups, and as a last-minute flavor enhancer. Refrigerate for up to 6 months.
SESAME SEED PASTE	Thick, strong-tasting paste made from toasted ground sesame seeds. Commonly used in meat marinades and as a sauce for cold plate dishes. Before using, dilute equal parts paste with water or oil.
SHRIMP, DRIED	Shelled, lightly salted, and dried tiny shrimp have a strong flavor which enhances vegetable dishes and soups. Soak in warm water for 10 to 15 minutes before using.
SOY SAUCE	Most naturally fermented soy sauces are made from soy beans, wheat flour, salt, and water. All-purpose, light, dark, and thick varieties are available in stores with varying amounts of salt. The all-purpose Kikkoman soy sauce is ideal for most Oriental dishes. For those on a reduced sodium diet, Kikkoman has a low sodium soy sauce with a salt content of only 7 to 8 percent. Purchase only naturally fermented types of soy sauce for all dishes prepared in this book.

SPRING ROLL WRAPPERS	White, paper-thin squares of pastry made from soft wheat flour and water. Sold fresh or frozen in Chinese markets. When deep-fried, they have a more delicate, crispier texture than egg roll skins. Avoid prolonged exposure to air—wrappers tend to dry out quickly if not covered. Freeze for up to 3 months.
STAR ANISE	Aromatic seed pod, shaped like an eight-pointed star, has strong licorice flavor. Used for stewing or braising, and in barbecue marinades.
STARCH	ALL-PURPOSE: For thickening sauces, cornstarch, tapioca starch, and arrowroot starch each produce clear, shiny sauces. Combine 1 part starch with 2 or 3 parts cold water and slowly add to cooking liquid. Cornstarch, used in meat marinades to help seal in juices, can also be used to coat meat before it is deep-fried. WHEAT STARCH: Starch removed from wheat flour after fermentation. Used to make a variety of dim sum wrappers.

Key for page 16

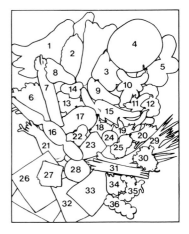

1) bok choy 2) Napa or Chinese cabbage 3) bitter melon 4) winter melon 5) fuzzy melon 6) fresh ginger root 7) Chinese white turnip 8) Shanghai bok choy 9) white eggplant 10) Oriental eggplant 11) chili peppers 12) green peppers 13) fresh water chestnuts 14) taro root 15) Chinese okra 16) lotus root 17) Chinese yard long beans 18) green beans 19) snow peas 20) fresh bean sprouts 21) Chinese yard long beans 22) fresh tomatoes 23) whole bamboo shoot 24) onion 25) heads of garlic 26) spring roll wrappers 27) wonton skins 28) pot sticker wrappers 29) green onions 30) cilantro or Chinese parsley 31) Chinese chives 32) Shanghai thick noodles 33) fresh egg noodles 34) baby corn 35) straw mushrooms 36) fresh quail eggs

Martin Yan, the Chinese Chef

Martin Yan, the Chinese Chef

SZECHUAN PEPPERCORNS	Tiny, reddish-brown berries with a pungent aroma. Before using, toast peppercorns to bring out their full flavor. In a wide frying pan, toast peppercorns over medium-high heat for 5 minutes or until fragrant, shaking pan frequently. If recipe requires ground toasted Szechuan peppercorns, use a mortar and pestle to grind to a powder.
SZECHUAN PRESERVED VEGETABLE	Hot, spicy pickled mustard green, widely used in a variety of northern-style dishes. Rinse off some of the red chili powder, if a milder flavor is desired, and thinly slice to use. Refrigerate in a tightly covered jar for up to 6 months.
TANGERINE PEEL	Dried peel from tangerine oranges with special fragrance and flavor; soak briefly before using in soups and in stewed or braised dishes.
TIGER LILY BUDS	Also called golden needles, these dried tiger lily buds are 2 to 3 inches long. They add a delicate sweet flavor and aroma to soup, poultry, fish, or meat. Before using, soak in warm water for 30 minutes; discard the hard tips.

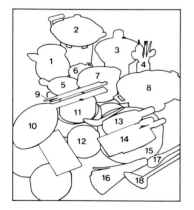

Key for page 17

1) large clay pot 2) spun-steel wok with lid 3) brass Mongolian firepot 4) chopsticks and small wire strainers 5) medium-size clay pot 6) small clay pot 7) 4-quart pot with steamer 8) Meyer electric wok with lid 9) long cooking chopsticks 10) large wire strainer 11) 10-inch bamboo steamer 12) 6-inch dim sum steamer 13) wooden moon cake mold 14) Chinese chopper and high-carbon Chinese cleaver 15) round wooden chopping block 16) bamboo brush for wok cleaning 17) wooden spatula 18) stainless steel spatula

Martin Yan, the Chinese Chef

TOFU	See Bean Curd, and page 79.
WATER CHESTNUTS	Tubers found on a common marsh plant. Crisp, crunchy texture with a slightly sweet flavor. Available canned, or fresh (around July to August) in some Chinese markets. Peel before using.
WINE	In Chinese cooking, different wines are used. Common varieties include: Shao Hsing, Fun Chin, or common rice wine. If Chinese wine is not available, dry sherry may be substituted. See also page 94.
WINTER MELON	A member of the muskmelon family, it has a thick, dark green skin and a white flesh that turns transparent when cooked. Lasts only a few days in the refrigerator when cut. Used in soups, and in stir-fried and casserole dishes.
WON TON WRAPPERS	Thin, 3-inch-square pieces of dough made from high-gluten flour, water, and eggs. Packed in 1-pound, airtight plastic bags, or fresh or frozen in Chinese markets. Wonton wrappers can be deep-fried, steamed, or boiled in soup. If frozen, thaw in package before using.

CHINESE UTENSILS & TOOLS

Only a few essential items are required for Chinese cooking: a wok, a curved spatula, and a sharp Chinese chef's knife. After you have been wokking for a while, you may wish to purchase a few other traditional utensils such as a set of bamboo steamers and a wire strainer. Of course, you can always improvise and use whatever utensils you have on hand, but as you cook more Chinese dishes for your family and friends, you might find it more exciting and handier to use the tools of the Chinese chef.

THE WOK

Chinese cuisine boasts some 80,000 dishes, and most of them are prepared in the wok, the single most important tool of the Chinese chef.

The wok, a round-bottomed, bowl-shaped pan, has been used for centuries in Chinese kitchens. Its unique shape arose out of necessity; the wok conducts heat very efficiently, economizing on often-scarce cooking fuel. The earliest woks were designed to fit into round fire pits.

Highly efficient in terms of kitchen space, the wok takes the place of dozens of pots and pans, and with it, almost any cooking method can be used and any ingredient cooked. A peek into any Chinese kitchen will show you that Chinese chefs and home cooks alike routinely use the wok to stir-fry, deep-fry, braise, simmer, stew, and steam.

Various types of woks are commercially available and usually come with a high dome-shaped cover (lid). Traditionally, woks were made of cast iron. Today, most woks are made of spun steel (carbon steel). Spun steel conducts heat evenly while allowing a "seasoned" layer of oil to adhere to the cooking surface. This protective layer keeps the food from sticking during the high-heat frying.

Woks are also made of aluminum and stainless steel—often with copper bottoms and sides to improve heat conduction—and are a good choice particularly for steaming and stewing.

If your preference is an electric wok, you can choose a model made from stainless steel or one with a non-stick finish inside. Because of the built-in heat control, an electric wok is ideal for deep-frying and is the perfect pan to use for table top cooking. The new models of electric woks, such as Meyer, are well designed and give very satisfactory results for stir-frying too.

Woks vary in shape and size. The traditional round-bottom ones can sit directly on a gas burner; the newer flat-bottom woks will remain stable on either a gas or an electric element. A 14-inch wok is the ideal size for the average family and will accommodate food for two to eight people.

The key to successful wok cooking is the proper care of the wok. These simple steps will ensure the best results: New woks should be scoured with hot, soapy water to remove any protective coating applied at the factory. Dry the wok thoroughly, rub some vegetable oil evenly into the cooking surface, and heat for 20 to 25 minutes over medium to medium-high heat until the surface of the wok turns brown. This builds the first layer of what will become a solid "seasoned" surface. (Since woks vary, follow manufacturer's instructions.) The trick to maintaining and building up this layer is to wash the wok with hot water after each use—never use soap—dry it, and rub in a bit of fresh oil, if it is not to be used every day.

CHINESE CHEF'S KNIFE—The Cleaver

The Chinese chef's knife is almost as indispensable to the Chinese cook as is the wok. And like the wok, this heavy, wide-bladed knife is multi-functional. You can use it to slice, dice, shred, and mince; to tenderize meat; and to crush. The broad blade also serves as a scoop to lift chopped food from cutting board to pan.

Paired with a good cutting board—one that is stationary and will not slide during use—the chef's knife will perform delicate slicing as easily as it will cut through bones.

Keep a sharp edge on your chef's knife and store it in its own protected place—not in a drawer of miscellany where the edge will be dulled by knocking against other tools. To preserve the handle, never soak a chef's knife in dishwater, and *never* put it in the dishwasher. Wipe the blade with a hot soapy cloth and rinse after each use, then wipe dry.

A Chinese chef's knife may feel large and awkward the first time you hold it. Go slowly while you develop your skill. Because the chef's knife is sharp and heavy you can slice meat and vegetables without exerting too much force. With a few weeks of practice you'll be able to do it with ease and pleasure.

TOOLS

Spatula: The metal Chinese spatula, sold with a wok set or separately, is a multi-purpose, long-handled tool that is curved to fit the sloping sides of the wok. This is the utensil you use for stir-frying; with it, you can quickly scoop up and toss meat and vegetables as they flash cook. Larger than the Western spatula or long-handled spoon (you can substitute these if you choose), the Chinese spatula is most compatible with the wok and does the job most efficiently.

Wire Strainer: The Chinese strainer is both handsome and practical. Made in the shape of a shallow ladle, it is used to lift out and drain foods from hot oil. As a substitute use a slotted spoon.

Steamer: There are two types of steamers available, bamboo and aluminum. The intriguing and traditional Chinese bamboo steamers come in a variety of sizes and will fit right inside a wok. For a 14-inch wok, buy a 13-inch steamer. The bamboo steamer allows slow dissipation of moisture through the lattice top which prevents excessive condensation of steam on your dish. Bamboo steamers are designed to stack one on top of the other, allowing several dishes to be cooked simultaneously.

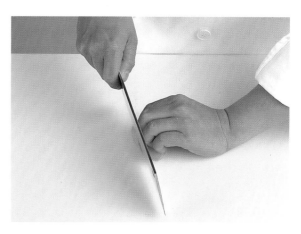

CLOCKWISE FROM TOP RIGHT: Correct hand position for holding a Chinese cleaver; slicing a lotus root; dicing a firm tomato; and mincing parsley.

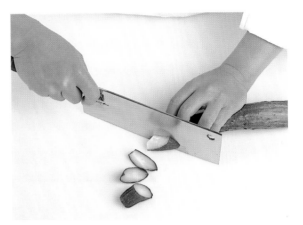

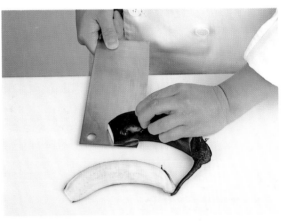

CLOCKWISE FROM TOP RIGHT: Roll cutting an Oriental cucumber; slant slicing an Oriental eggplant; crushing cloves of garlic; shredding Chinese cabbage; and julienne cutting a red pepper.

Martin Yan, the Chinese Chef

CUTTING TECHNIQUES

Holding the Cleaver: Hold the handle of the chef's knife in your writing hand and slide your hand forward just until your thumb reaches one side of the blade and your index finger is on the other side. Grasp the handle tightly. With four fingers of your free hand curved downward and inward, hold the food to be cut. The first knuckle serves as a cutting guide, with the chef's knife placed so the flat side of the blade is just touching it. Never stretch your fingers outward toward the blade, and never lift the cutting edge of the chef's knife higher than the level of your knuckle.

Slicing: This technique is used to cut meat or vegetables into the desired size, depending on the instructions of each recipe. Hold the food firmly on the cutting board with the curled fingers of your free hand placed perpendicular to the blade. Cut straight down with the Chinese chef's knife.

Cubing or Dicing: After you have sliced an ingredient into long slices or sticks, stack slices and cut across stacks perpendicularly to make cubes. The size of the cube is determined by the thickness of the first slice. In the recipes, "diced" means ¼- to ½-inch squares; "cubes" are larger.

Mincing: To achieve this "minced" size easily, sliver the ingredient into thin strips. Resting the tip of the chef's knife on the cutting board and holding onto the handle with one hand, while holding down the tip of the blunt edge with your other hand, move knife blade up and down in a chopping motion. Using the tip as a pivot, move the knife from side to side to mince all little pieces. Occasionally scoop everything into a pile and continue to mince for finer pieces.

Roll Cutting: This is used to cut long vegetables such as carrots or zucchini. Hold the ingredient with your free hand and cut a diagonal slice at the tip. Roll the ingredient a quarter turn, then cut again at the same angle. Continue turning and cutting until you reach the final cut.

Slivers (shredding): This is the most common technique used in Chinese cooking. Use it to cut ingredients into uniform thin strips. Thinly slice the ingredient first, then stack pieces and cut vertically through the stack, into very thin strips, smaller than matchstick pieces.

Horizontal/Slant Slicing: Hold the piece of food firmly on the cutting board with the fingers of your free hand flat on top. Angle the chef's knife almost parallel to the board and slightly downward. Move the blade in a back and forth slicing motion.

Chopping: Most Chinese chef's knives are designed for slicing and cutting; you need a heavy-duty chopper to cut through large bones. To cut spareribs into shorter lengths, for example, chop with a hard, straight downward motion; never jiggle the blade from side to side. If the bone is not cleanly cut, Chinese chefs hammer down on the top blunt edge of the chopper with their fists until the blade is forced through.

Matchstick or Julienne Cutting: Cut the ingredient into ¼-inch thick pieces, stack the pieces, and cut vertically through the stack, to about the size of wooden matchstick pieces (about ¼-inch wide).

Crushing: This technique is most often used with garlic or ginger. Place a garlic clove or slice of ginger on the cutting board, then hold the chef's knife, blade facing away, horizontally on top of the food. Whack the broad side of the blade with the heel of the palm of your free hand to crush the food underneath.

COOKING TECHNIQUES

Stir-Frying

The most common technique of cooking Chinese food is the stir-fry method. This process is simple, quick and requires little special effort. A wok or a wide frying pan is heated over a high temperature until hot. Oil is added, and the wok is swirled to coat the sides. Then minced garlic and/or ginger are added and stir-fried until fragrant. The remaining ingredients, meat, seafood, or vegetables, are then added according to their length of cooking time, with ingredients that take the longest added first. All ingredients should be cut into uniform shapes and sizes to ensure even cooking. Since this type of cooking is done over high heat, it is necessary to rapidly stir ingredients to prevent over-cooking or burning; hence the name stir-fry. Stir-frying is fun, quick, and this technique preserves nutrients and flavor.

Smoking

Chinese chefs use smoke-cooking as a flavoring technique. Meats are slowly cooked in a large oven that contains black tea leaves and/or camphor chips. However, smoking can be easily accomplished in a foil-lined wok. The meat should first be partially cooked or steamed. Before smoking, sprinkle black tea leaves, camphor chips, and brown sugar (uncooked rice is often used with the mixture for added aroma) over the bottom of the wok. Place the meat on a rack in the wok, cover, then quickly heat. The smoke will permeate the meat imparting a robust, smoky flavor.

Blanching

Water blanching is a simple technique, used primarily for vegetables. Food is dipped in boiling water for a couple of minutes, then removed and rinsed under cold water.

Oil blanching is the Chinese technique of blanching bite-size pieces of meat or seafood in moderately hot oil (300-325°F), in order to seal in juices. Though traditionally used in Chinese restaurants before stir-frying to give a shiny finish and ensure uniform cooking, this is not a practical method for home use.

Roasting

In China, roasting refers to slowly cooking large quantities of meat over a wood-burning fire. The meat is roasted on a hook, allowing the heat to evenly circulate around the meat. This roasting method is popular in Chinese restaurants, but is rarely done in the home. In the West, our ovens can do the same job. Place the meat on a rack set in a foil-lined baking pan. Roast for the specified amount of time, basting with excess pan juices, turning meat occasionally.

Steaming

Steaming is the method used to cook food over, rather than in, boiling water. It is a simple and nutritious way to prepare foods. Steaming is often used as a preparatory step before smoking or frying whole meats.

Pour water into a wok to a depth of 2 inches. Place a bamboo steamer, cake rack, or criss-crossed chopsticks over the water (not in). Cover with wok lid and bring water to a boil (the bamboo steamer comes with its own lid). Place the food in a heatproof dish that fits in the steamer or wok. Cover and maintain heat to keep water boiling. Occasionally check water level by carefully lifting lid so the steam rises away from you. Add water when necessary.

When steaming dim sum, line the bottom of a bamboo steamer with a small damp cloth to prevent dim sum from sticking to the steamer. Arrange dim sum on the cloth, cover, and place steamer over boiling water in a wok.

Deep-Frying

Deep-frying is the cooking of food while totally submerged in hot oil. To achieve crispy deep-fried food, it is important to maintain the temperature of the oil. When the oil is not hot enough, the food cooks too slowly and absorbs oil, resulting in greasy food. If the oil is too hot, the food will brown too quickly, leaving the inside raw. To ensure even temperature control, use a deep-frying thermometer. When deep-frying food, use a flat-bottom wok or a wok set in a ring stand to prevent the wok from tipping. Pour oil into a wok to a depth of 1½ to 2 inches. Heat oil to the specified temperature. Carefully slide food, a few pieces at a time, into oil. Turn frequently until done. (Adding too much food at once will lower the temperature of the oil.) Lift out fried food with a slotted spoon or a wire strainer. Drain on paper towels.

Simmering

Simmering is a technique of gently cooking food just below the boiling point in enough liquid to cover it. Simmering is often used to make broths, stews, or sauces.

Braising

Braising is a combined technique of stir-frying and stewing. The meat is first browned to seal in natural juices. It is then covered and cooked in liquid ingredients over low heat until tender, allowing the flavors of the sauce to permeate the meat.

Red Cooking

Red-cooking is the Chinese technique of slow-cooking with a sauce, similar to the Western stewing. The meat is browned to seal in the natural juices, then cooked in a sauce usually containing dark soy sauce, which gives a rich, reddish-brown color.

SAUCES/CONDIMENTS

ALL-PURPOSE BATTER

Combine ¾ **cup flour, 1¼ teaspoons baking powder,** and ½ **teaspoon sugar;** mix well. Slowly add ⅔ **cup water.** Blend in ½ **teaspoon vegetable oil** with wire whisk until smooth. Let set 15 minutes before using.

BASIC STEW SAUCE

Combine **3 cups water,** ½ **cup soy sauce,** ⅓ **cup dark soy sauce,** ¼ **cup dry sherry, 4 cloves minced garlic, 2 whole star anise, 3 tablespoons sugar,** and **2 tablespoons vegetable oil** in saucepan. Bring to boil, then reduce heat, cover, and simmer for 20 minutes, stirring occasionally. Strain liquid and use in braised, stewed, and casserole dishes.

BLACK BEAN SAUCE

Rinse ¼ **cup fermented black beans;** drain. Mash beans in a bowl. Place wok over medium heat until hot. Add **2 tablespoons vegetable oil.** Add **3 cloves minced garlic;** cook until fragrant. Add black beans, **3 tablespoons dry sherry, 2 tablespoons dark soy sauce, 1 tablespoon brown sugar,** and **2 teaspoons sesame oil;** cook, stirring, for 2 to 3 minutes. Use in steamed, stir-fried, or braised dishes.

CHILI OIL

Heat ¾ **cup vegetable oil** over high heat until oil reaches about 375°F. Remove from heat; add **2 teaspoons crushed red chili peppers** and ½ **teaspoon sesame oil.** Let cool. Use as dip or use few drops to add zest to any dish.

FIVE-SPICE SALT

Place ¼ **cup salt** and ¾ **teaspoon Chinese five-spice** in wok over medium heat, swirling wok, for 2 to 3 minutes. Let cool. Use as seasoning salt for poultry and seafood dishes.

GINGER & GREEN ONION DIP

Heat ⅓ **cup vegetable oil** over medium-high heat until oil reaches about 350°F. Remove from heat; add **3 tablespoons slivered green onions, 1 tablespoon slivered fresh ginger,** and ½ **teaspoon salt;** mix well. Serve hot as dip for poultry and steamed fish dishes.

HOT MUSTARD SAUCE

Combine **2 tablespoons hot mustard powder, 2 tablespoons water,** and ⅛ **teaspoon sesame oil** in a bowl; stir to smooth paste. Set aside for 1 hour.

KUNG PAO SAUCE

In saucepan, combine ½ **cup soy sauce, 2 tablespoons rice vinegar, 1 tablespoon sugar, 1 tablespoon minced green onion, 2 teaspoons chili oil, 1½ teaspoons sesame oil, ¼ teaspoon ground toasted Szechuan peppercorns,** and **2 cloves minced garlic.** Bring to boil, then reduce heat to medium and cook for 2 minutes. Let cool. Use as all-purpose seasoning sauce.

PLUM SAUCE

In food processor, combine **½ cup crushed pineapple, ⅓ cup mashed, seeded Chinese salted plums, ¼ cup pineapple juice, ¼ cup brown sugar, 3 tablespoons cider vinegar, 3 tablespoons apricot preserves,** and **2 cloves minced garlic.** Whirl to smooth paste. Transfer to saucepan; add **1 teaspoon crushed red chili peppers.** Bring to boil, reduce heat, and simmer 5 minutes, stirring constantly. Use as seasoning sauce in steamed or braised meat and poultry dishes.

SWEET & SOUR SAUCE

Combine **1 tablespoon cornstarch** and **⅓ cup water** in saucepan. Stir in **6 tablespoons brown sugar, ¼ cup rice vinegar, ¼ cup orange juice, 3 tablespoons ketchup, 2 tablespoons lemon juice, 1 tablespoon lime juice, 2 teaspoons soy sauce, ½ teaspoon minced fresh ginger, ¼ teaspoon chili oil, ¼ teaspoon Tabasco sauce,** and **1 tablespoon shredded pickled ginger.** Cook over medium heat, stirring, until sauce boils and thickens. Serve as dip.

SZECHUAN PEPPERCORN SALT

Place **¼ cup salt** and **¾ teaspoon ground toasted Szechuan peppercorns** in wok over medium heat, swirling wok, for 2 to 3 minutes. Let cool. Use as seasoning salt for meat and seafood dishes.

CANTON

The flavors of Canton combine in a subtle, natural style of cooking that utilize both fresh and exotic ingredients in a variety of interesting dishes.

CLOCKWISE FROM TOP RIGHT: Baked Pork Buns (page 43); Taro Dumplings (page 41); Har Gow (page 39); and Four-Color Siu Mai (page 40); basket of fresh lychee; Eight Precious Duck (page 59); Eight Treasure Winter Melon Soup (page 49); Seaweed Rolls (page 44); and carved winter melon.

I was born in the lush province of Guangdong, known for its rich agriculture and thriving port. The capital city of this subtropical region is Guangzhou (Canton), a bustling port city long known as a culinary center.

Guangzhou has more restaurants than any other city in China due to the availability of a wide range of fresh and often exotic foods. A staggering number of recipes originate from Guangzhou because of the plentiful ingredients in the area.

The benevolent environment of Guangzhou boasts exotic fruits such as lychees and longans, plus citrus fruits, bananas, and melons, as well as mushrooms and the widest range of vegetables cultivated. It is also known as one of China's "rice bowls," the moist climate allowing that staple to flourish.

The cuisine of Guangzhou is well known to most of us, primarily because most of the Chinese who immigrated to America in the late 19th and early 20th centuries came from Guangdong province.

The cuisine of Guangzhou is a fresh, natural cooking style which takes full advantage of the flavors of fresh ingredients to give each dish its character. It is a much subtler approach to flavor than the condiment-oriented cooking of some of the other regional cuisines.

The cooking of the South is known for its diversity. For example, *dim sum*, the tantalizing snacks famous for their wide range of tastes, ingredients, and methods of preparation, are said to have reached perfection in Guangzhou's innumerable teahouses. Main dishes are equally varied in ingredients and preparation techniques. Southern chefs fry, roast, steam, saute, barbecue, and braise an astounding array of meats, poultry, and seafoods.

South China is famed for fresh, delicately prepared foods, with great importance placed on the appearance of the finished dish. Ingredients are chosen so that flavors and colors will either complement or contrast, depending on the desired effect. The southern approach to cuisine assures that the final product will be an all-around triumph.

SUGGESTED MENUS

Eight Treasure Winter Melon Soup
Sizzling Black Bean Chicken
Sea Harvest in a Nest
Almond Tea

Crab & Bean Curd Soup
Twin Mushrooms
Eight Precious Duck
Sweet Water Chestnut Soup

Seaweed Rolls
Steamed Sea Bass
Salt-Baked Chicken
Sweet Rice Balls

Chinese BBQ Pork
Shrimp-Filled Delicacies
Curried Rice Stick Noodles
Crispy Nut Pockets

Canton

CHINESE BBQ PORK

Makes: 6 to 8 servings
Cooking time: 1¼ hours

1 boneless pork shoulder or butt (about 3 pounds)

Marinade

¼ cup *each* hoisin sauce and soy sauce

3 tablespoons dry sherry

2 tablespoons *each* ketchup and sugar

1 clove garlic, minced

1 tablespoon grated orange peel

1 tablespoon sesame seed paste (optional)

1 teaspoon *each* minced fresh ginger and sesame oil

½ teaspoon Chinese five-spice

4 or 5 drops red food color (optional)

Preparation

Trim and discard excess fat from pork. Then cut pork into 3- by 8- by 1-inch pieces. Combine marinade ingredients in a large bowl. Add pork; stir to coat. Cover and refrigerate for at least 2 to 4 hours or overnight, turning occasionally.

Cooking

Remove pork from marinade (reserve marinade) and arrange in a single layer on a rack over a large foil-lined baking pan. Bake, uncovered, in a 350°F oven for 30 minutes. Turn pork slices over and continue to bake for 45 more minutes, brushing occasionally with reserved marinade.

Cut into thin slices; serve hot or cold.

Tips

Substitute 3 pounds pork spareribs for boneless pork shoulder. Follow same procedure.

For a more exotic flavor, add 2 tablespoons mashed red fermented bean curd to the marinade. Reduce soy sauce to 1 tablespoon. A well-marbled pork shoulder will give the juiciest result.

Chinese BBQ Pork is a common ingredient in many Chinese dishes (such as Baked Pork Buns, page 43). You may want to prepare a double recipe and keep it on hand in the freezer.

Martin Yan, the Chinese Chef

HAR GOW

Makes: 30 dumplings
Cooking time: 40 minutes

Filling

- ¾ pound medium-size raw shrimp, shelled, deveined, and coarsely chopped
- ¼ cup finely chopped bamboo shoots
- 1 egg white
- 1 tablespoon cornstarch
- 1 teaspoon *each* sesame oil and dry sherry
- ¾ teaspoon salt
- Dash of white pepper

Dough

- 1 cup wheat starch
- ⅓ cup cornstarch
- ¼ teaspoon salt
- 1 cup boiling water
- 1½ tablespoons vegetable oil, lard or shortening

  Soy Sauce, for dipping

  Homemade Chili Oil, for dipping (page 32)

Preparation

Combine filling ingredients in a bowl; mix well. Set aside.

Measure wheat starch, cornstarch, and salt into a bowl. Mix in boiling water, stirring with chopsticks or a fork until dough is evenly moistened. Cover and let rest for 15 to 20 minutes.

On a lightly floured surface, knead dough until smooth. Gradually work oil in, kneading to blend after each addition, until dough glistens and feels satiny. Divide dough in half. Roll each half into a 15-inch-long cylinder. Cut each cylinder crosswise into 1-inch pieces; shape each piece into a ball.

To shape each dumpling, flatten one ball of dough with a rolling pin to make a 3 to 3½-inch circle, keeping remaining dough covered to prevent drying. Press edges of the circle firmly with your fingers to thin dough out. Place 1 teaspoon of filling in center of each circle. Fold circle in half over filling to form a semicircle. Pinch curved edges together, pleating one side to the other to seal. Finally, cover filled dumplings with a damp cloth while shaping remaining dumplings.

Cooking

Line the bottom of a steamer with a small damp cloth. Arrange dumplings, without crowding, on cloth. Cover and steam over boiling water for 18 to 20 minutes or until dumplings are translucent. Serve dumplings hot or cold, with soy sauce and chili oil.

Tips

Wheat starch is an essential ingredient in these dumplings, giving the wrappers a translucent appearance. Look for it in Chinese grocery stores.

Pictured on page 35

FOUR-COLOR SIU MAI

Makes: 30 to 32 dumplings
Cooking time: 40 minutes

Filling

- ½ pound ground lean beef
- 2 ounces medium-size raw shrimp, shelled and deveined
- 1 slice lean bacon or Chinese sausage, coarsely chopped
- 1 tablespoon chopped cilantro (Chinese parsley) leaves
- 2½ tablespoons cornstarch
- 1 teaspoon dry sherry
- ¾ teaspoon *each* salt and sesame oil
- ¼ teaspoon sugar

Toppings

- 5 dried black mushrooms
- 1½ teaspoons vegetable oil
- 1 egg, lightly beaten
- ¼ pound spinach leaves
- ¼ cup minced ham
- 30 to 32 pot stickers (or siu mai) wrappers
- Soy sauce, for dipping
- Hot Chinese Mustard, for dipping (page 32)

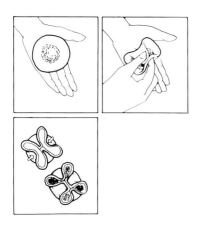

Preparation

In a food processor or blender, whirl filling ingredients into a smooth paste. Transfer to a bowl and set aside.

Soak mushrooms in enough warm water to cover for 30 minutes; drain. Cut off and discard stems; finely chop caps. Set aside.

Place a wide frying pan with a nonstick finish over medium-high heat until hot. Add oil, swirling to coat sides. Pour in egg, tilting pan to coat bottom evenly. Cook just until egg is set and feels dry on top. Remove from pan and let cool slightly. Finely chop egg and set aside.

Blanch spinach leaves in boiling water for 1 minute. Rinse under cold running water; drain well, and cool. Squeeze out all excess liquid from spinach, then finely chop. Set aside.

To fill each dumpling, spoon 1 heaping teaspoon of filling into center of each wrapper, keeping remaining wrappers covered to prevent drying (see illustration), Pinch opposite sides of wrapper together in the center. Pinch remaining sides together in the center to form 4 small pouches, using your fingers to slightly open pouches. Drop a small amount of mushroom in one pouch. Continue filling remaining 3 pouches respectively with egg, spinach, and ham. Cover filled dumplings with a damp cloth while filling remaining wrappers.

Cooking

Line the bottom of a steamer with a small damp cloth. Arrange dumplings, without crowding, on cloth. Cover and steam over boiling water for about 20 minutes or until meat is no longer pink. Serve with soy sauce and mustard.

Tips

Substitute other colorful Siu Mai toppings such as blanched carrots, bok choy, red peppers, and yellow zucchini.

Substitute won ton wrappers for the pot sticker wrappers trimming edges of wonton wrappers to

Martin Yan, the Chinese Chef

form circles. Cover with a damp cloth until ready to use.

Unlike stir-frying, which demands your undivided attention, steam-cooking takes care of itself. Just be sure to begin with enough water to last the full cooking time.

Pictured on page 35

TARO DUMPLINGS

Makes: 12 dumplings
Cooking time: 17 minutes

Pork Mixture

3 dried black mushrooms

¼ pound ground lean pork

2 teaspoons *each* soy sauce, dry sherry, and cornstarch

⅛ teaspoon salt

Sauce

1 tablespoon *each* oyster sauce and soy sauce

1 teaspoon sesame oil

½ teaspoon sugar
Dash of white pepper

1 teaspoon cornstarch mixed with 2 teaspoons water

Preparation

Soak mushrooms in enough warm water to cover for 30 minutes; drain. Cut off and discard hard stems. Mince caps and combine with remaining pork mixture ingredients in a bowl; mix well and set aside.

Combine sauce ingredients in a bowl and set aside.

Place taro in a heatproof dish. Set dish in a steamer or on a rack in a wok. Cover and steam over boiling water for 25 minutes or until tender. Transfer taro to a large bowl and mash until smooth. Add cornstarch, shortening, sugar, and salt; blend well to make a smooth dough. (If dough is too dry, add a few drops of boiling water.)

On a lightly floured surface, knead dough for 5 minutes or until smooth. Cover with a damp cloth and let rest for 10 minutes.

(continued on next page)

(continued from previous page)

Dough

- 1 pound taro, peeled and cut into ¼-inch-thick slices
- ¼ cup cornstarch
- 6 tablespoons solid vegetable shortening or lard
- 1½ teaspoons sugar
- ½ teaspoon salt

- 1½ teaspoons vegetable oil
- 2 ounces medium-size raw shrimp, shelled, deveined, and coarsely chopped
- 2 tablespoons coarsely chopped bamboo shoots

  Vegetable oil for deep-frying

Cooking

Place a wok or wide frying pan over high heat until hot. Add oil, swirling to coat sides. Add pork mixture; stir and toss for 2 minutes. Add shrimp; stir-fry for 1½ to 2 minutes or until shrimp turns pink. Add bamboo shoots and sauce; cook, stirring, until sauce boils and thickens. Let cool.

Divide dough in half. With greased hands, form dough into a 16-inch-long cylinder. Cut into 1-inch pieces. To make dumplings, flatten one piece of dough into a 2½-inch-diameter circle, keeping remaining dough covered to prevent drying. Place 1 level teaspoon of pork mixture in center of each circle. Fold in half over filling to form a semicircle, pressing edges to seal. Cover filled dumplings with a damp cloth while filling remaining dumplings.

Set wok in a ring stand and add oil to a depth of 2 inches. Place oil over medium-high heat until oil reaches about 325°F. Add dumplings, a few at a time, and deep-fry for about 3 to 4 minutes or until golden brown, turning frequently. Lift out and drain on paper towels. Keep warm in a 200°F oven while cooking remaining dumplings. Serve hot.

Martin Yan, the Chinese Chef

BAKED PORK BUNS

Makes: 12 buns
Cooking time: 30 minutes

Dough

4 tablespoons sugar
½ cup warm milk (110°F)
⅓ cup warm water (110°F)
2 teaspoons active dry yeast
2 to 2½ cups all-purpose flour
Dash of salt

Filling

8 to 10 dried black mushrooms
2 tablespoons vegetable oil
½ cup minced green onions (including tops)
2 cloves garlic, minced
½ cup water
4 teaspoons *each* hoisin sauce and oyster sauce
1 tablespoon sugar
2 teaspoons cornstarch mixed with 1 tablespoon water
1½ cups chopped Chinese BBQ Pork (page 38)

1 egg yolk, lightly beaten

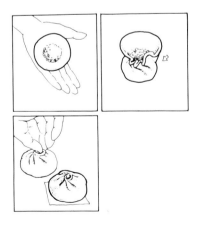

Preparation

In a large bowl, dissolve 2 tablespoons of the sugar in milk and water. Sprinkle yeast over top of milk mixture and let stand at room temperature for 10 minutes or until frothy. Gradually mix in remaining 2 tablespoons sugar, flour, and salt.

On a lightly floured surface, knead dough for about 5 minutes or until smooth and elastic. Shape into a ball and place in a lightly greased bowl. Cover with a damp cloth and let rise in a warm area for about 1 hour or until doubled.

Meanwhile, soak mushrooms in enough warm water to cover for 30 minutes; drain. Cut off and discard stems; coarsely chop caps. Set aside.

Cooking

Place wok or wide frying pan over high heat until hot. Add oil, swirling to coat sides. Add green onions, garlic, and mushrooms; stir-fry for 1 minute. Stir in water, hoisin sauce, oyster sauce, and sugar; mix well. Add cornstarch solution and cook, stirring, until sauce boils and thickens. Add pork; mix well. Remove from heat and let cool.

Punch down dough, then roll on a lightly floured surface into a 12-inch-long cylinder. Cut cylinder crosswise into 1-inch pieces. Shape each piece into a ball; let rest for 5 minutes.

To shape each dumpling, flatten one ball with a rolling pin to make a 4- to 6-inch circle, keeping dough covered to prevent drying. Place 1 heaping tablespoon of filling in center of each circle. (see illustration) Gather edges of circle over filling; close top by pleating, pinching, and twisting edges together. Place buns, pleated side down, on a baking sheet, allowing enough room for rising. Cover with a damp cloth and let rise in a warm place for about 30 minutes or until light and puffy. Brush tops of buns with egg yolk. Let rise for 15 more minutes.

Bake in a 350°F oven for 18 to 20 minutes or until golden brown.

(continued on next page)

(continued from previous page)

Tips

Traditionally, these buns are steamed over boiling water, pleated side up, for 12 to 15 minutes rather than baked. Follow same procedure for preparing dough except do not brush tops of buns with egg yolk.

Try other fillings, such as minced pork, chicken or shrimp.

SEAWEED ROLLS

Makes: 12 rolls
Cooking time: 6 to 8 minutes

   6 dried black mushrooms
   3 green onions (including tops)
   2 ounces Smithfield or Virginia ham
   ½ small cucumber, peeled and seeded

Paste

   1 whole chicken breast, skinned, boned, and cut into 2-inch pieces
   1 egg white
   1 tablespoon dry sherry
   4 teaspoons cornstarch
   ½ teaspoon salt
     Dash of white pepper

   3 sheets seaweed (nori), cut into 3- to 3 ½-inch squares

     Vegetable oil for deep-frying

Preparation

Soak mushrooms in enough warm water to cover for 30 minutes; drain. Cut off and discard stems, thinly slice caps.

Cut green onions diagonally into 3½-inch pieces. Cut ham and cucumber into 3½-inch matchstick pieces.

In a food processor or blender, whirl paste ingredients until smooth; remove to a bowl.

Spread 1 level tablespoon of paste evenly over entire surface of each seaweed square. Place 1 piece each of green onion, ham, and cucumber, and 2 pieces of mushroom along the center of seaweed square. Beginning at one end, roll seaweed to make a ¾-inch-diameter cylinder. Remove to a plate and set aside while filling remaining seaweed rolls.

Cooking

Set wok in a ring stand and add oil to a depth of 1½ to 2 inches. Place over medium-high until oil reaches about 350°F. Add rolls, a few at a time, and deep-fry for 1½ to 2 minutes, turning occasionally. Lift out and drain on paper towels. Keep warm while cooking remaining rolls. Cut each roll diagonally in half. Serve hot.

Tips

Substitute ½ pound raw shrimp, shelled and deveined for the chicken breast. Follow the same procedure.

Pictured on page 34

Martin Yan, the Chinese Chef

CLASSIC WONTONS

Makes: 6 to 7 dozen wontons
Cooking time: 1 hour

Filling

    1 bunch spinach (about 1
      pound)
    ¾ pound ground lean pork
    ¼ pound ground lean beef
    ¼ cup finely chopped water
      chestnuts
    2 tablespoons minced green
      onion (including top)
1 to 2 tablespoons chicken broth
    1 tablespoon oyster sauce
    1 egg white
    2 teaspoons cornstarch
    1 teaspoon *each* sesame oil
      and dry sherry
    ¼ teaspoon salt

    1 package (about 1 pound)
      wonton wrappers
    1 egg, lightly beaten

      Vegetable oil for deep-
      frying

      Sweet & Sour Sauce,
      for dipping (page 33)

Preparation

Wash spinach thoroughly; cut off and discard stems. Blanch spinach in a large pot of boiling water for 2 minutes. Rinse under cold running water; drain and let cool. Squeeze out all excess liquid from spinach, then coarsely chop.

Combine spinach with remaining filling ingredients in a large bowl; mix well.

To fill each wonton, place 1 heaping teaspoon of filling in center of each wonton wrapper, keeping remaining wrappers covered to prevent drying. Brush edges of wonton lightly with egg. Fold in half over filling to form a triangle, pressing edges firmly together to seal. Place filled wontons on a plate and cover with a damp cloth while filling remaining wontons.

Cooking

Set wok in a ring stand and add oil to a depth of 2 inches. Place over medium-high heat until oil reaches about 350°F. Add wontons, a few at a time, and deep-fry for 3 to 3½ minutes or until golden brown, turning occasionally. Lift out and drain on paper towels. Keep warm in a 200°F oven while cooking remaining won tons. Serve hot with sweet and sour sauce.

Tips

Once wontons are wrapped, you can deep-fry them, add them to soup, or boil them in broth.

TWIN MUSHROOMS

Makes: 6 to 8 servings
Cooking time: 20 minutes

12 large dried black
mushrooms

Braising Sauce

⅔ cup chicken broth
3 tablespoons dry sherry
2 tablespoons oyster sauce
1 tablespoon soy sauce

Filling

¼ pound ground lean pork
¼ pound medium-size raw
shrimp, shelled and
deveined
3 water chestnuts
1 egg white
2 teaspoons *each* sesame oil
and cornstarch
½ teaspoon *each* salt and
minced fresh ginger
Dash of white pepper

12 large fresh mushroom
caps
3 tablespoons vegetable oil
1½ teaspoons cornstarch
mixed with 1 tablespoon
water
1 tablespoon cilantro
(Chinese parsley) leaves,
for garnish

Preparation

Soak dried mushrooms in enough warm water to cover for 30 minutes; drain. Cut off and discard stems. Set caps aside.

In a small bowl, combine braising sauce ingredients; mix well and set aside.

In a food processor or blender, whirl filling ingredients into a smooth paste. Mound about 1½ teaspoons of filling in each fresh mushroom cap and in each soaked black mushroom cap, using a knife to smooth top of mound evenly.

Cooking

Place a wok or wide frying pan over medium heat until hot. Add 1½ tablespoons of the oil, swirling to coat sides. Arrange half the mushrooms, filling side down, in wok and cook for about 1½ minutes on each side or until lightly browned. Swirl wok to ensure even browning. Pour half the braising sauce over mushrooms. Reduce heat, cover, and simmer for 5 minutes. Add half the cornstarch solution and cook, stirring, until sauce boils and thickens. Remove mushrooms and sauce to a dish and keep warm.

Wipe wok clean, then cook remaining mushrooms, using remaining 1½ tablespoons oil, braising sauce, and cornstarch solution.

To serve, place half the mushrooms, filling side up, in the center of a platter. Surround with remaining mushrooms, filling side down. Garnish with cilantro leaves.

Tips

Mushroom caps can be stuffed up to a day in advance; refrigerate until ready to use. Cook mushrooms just before serving.

Pictured on page 54

Martin Yan, The Chinese Chef

CRABMEAT & BEAN CURD SOUP

Makes: 6 servings
Cooking time: 10 minutes

- 6 cups Basic Chicken Broth (page 106)
- 3 thin slices fresh ginger, each 1 by 2 inches
- 2 ounces Smithfield or Virginia ham, cut into matchstick pieces
- 1 small cucumber, peeled, seeded, and cut into matchstick pieces
- ¼ pound cooked crabmeat, shredded
- 1 package (about 1 pound) soft tofu (bean curd), drained and cut into ½-inch cubes
- 3 tablespoons cornstarch mixed with 3 tablespoons water
- 2 egg whites, lightly beaten
- 1 teaspoon sesame oil
  Dash of white pepper
  Salt

  Cilantro (Chinese parsley) sprigs, for garnish

Cooking

In a large pot, bring broth and ginger to a boil over high heat. Cook for 2 minutes, then remove and discard ginger. Add ham and cucumber and cook for 1 minute. Reduce heat to medium-low; add crabmeat and tofu and cook for 1 minute. Add cornstarch solution and cook, stirring, until soup boils and thickens slightly.

Remove from heat and slowly drizzle in egg whites, stirring constantly. Season soup with sesame oil, white pepper, and salt to taste. Garnish with cilantro. Serve immediately.

Tips
Soft tofu is fragile so handle with care.
If soft tofu is unavailable, use firm tofu.

Canton

CANTONESE SOUP WITH DUMPLINGS

Makes: 6 to 8 servings
Cooking time: 20 minutes

Filling

4 dried black mushrooms

2 tablespoons dried shrimp

¼ pound medium-size raw shrimp, shelled, deveined, and coarsely chopped

¼ pound boneless lean pork, diced

¼ cup coarsely chopped bamboo shoots

2 green onions (including tops), minced

1 egg, lightly beaten

2 tablespoons cornstarch

1 tablespoon *each* soy sauce and chopped cilantro (Chinese parsley) leaves

2 teaspoons sesame oil

½ teaspoon salt

28 to 32 pot sticker wrappers

1 egg yolk, lightly beaten

8 cups Basic Chicken Broth (page 106)
Salt

2 green onions (including tops), cut into 2-inch slivers, for garnish

Cilantro (Chinese parsley) sprigs, for garnish

Preparation

Soak mushrooms in enough warm water to cover for 30 minutes; drain. Soak dried shrimp in enough warm water to cover for 30 minutes; drain. Cut off and discard mushroom stems. Coarsely chop mushroom caps and dried shrimp.

In a medium-size bowl, combine mushrooms and dried shrimp with remaining filling ingredients; mix well.

To fill dumplings, place one heaping tablespoon filling in center of each wrapper, keeping remaining wrappers covered to prevent drying. Moisten edges of wrapper lightly with egg yolk. Fold wrapper in half over filling, pressing edges together to form a semicircle. Cover filled dumplings with a damp cloth while filling remaining wrappers.

Cooking

Bring broth to a boil in a large pot; salt to taste. Keep warm.

In another large pot, bring 8 cups of water to a boil. Add dumplings, without crowding, stirring to separate. When water returns to a boil, add 1½ cups cold water. Return to a boil again and cook, stirring, until dumplings start to float. Lift out dumplings with a wire strainer and place in individual soup bowls (about 4 dumplings per bowl). Return broth to a boil, then pour over dumplings. Sprinkle with green onion slivers and cilantro. Serve immediately.

Martin Yan, The Chinese Chef

EIGHT TREASURE WINTER MELON SOUP

Makes: 6 to 8 servings
Cooking time: 25 minutes

6 large dried black
  mushrooms

Marinade

1 tablespoon soy sauce

2 teaspoons dry sherry

½ teaspoon *each* salt and
  cornstarch

1 whole chicken breast,
  skinned, boned and cut
  into ½-inch cubes

¼ pound boneless lean pork,
  cut into ½-inch cubes

6 cups Basic Chicken Broth
  (page 106)

½ pound winter melon,
  hard skin cut off, cut into
  ½-inch cubes

2 ounces cooked crabmeat,
  shredded

⅓ pound medium-size raw
  shrimp, shelled, deveined,
  and coarsely chopped

1 ounce Smithfield or
  Virginia ham, diced

¼ cup *each* canned straw
  mushrooms and frozen
  peas, thawed

1 egg white, lightly beaten
  (optional)

¼ teaspoon sesame oil
  Dash of white pepper

Preparation

Soak mushrooms in enough warm water to cover for 30 minutes; drain. Cut off and discard stems; coarsely chop caps. Set aside.

In a large bowl, combine marinade ingredients. Add chicken and pork; stir to coat. Set aside for 30 minutes.

Cooking

In a large pot, bring broth to a boil over high heat. Add black mushrooms and melon; reduce heat, cover, and simmer for 12 to 15 minutes or until melon begins to turn transparent. Increase heat to medium-high and return broth to a boil. Stir in chicken and pork; cook for 3 minutes. Add crabmeat, shrimp, ham, straw mushrooms and peas; cook, stirring, for 1 to 2 minutes.

Remove from heat. If desired, gradually drizzle in egg white, stirring constantly. Stir in sesame oil and white pepper. Serve soup in a large tureen or individual soup bowls.

Tips

This is a classic banquet dish which is usually served in a carved winter melon.

You can buy winter melon by the pound in Oriental markets.

An uncut whole winter melon can be kept in a dry, cool place for several months.

Pictured on page 34

Canton

If you are new to Chinese cooking, it's easiest to become acquainted with the recipes in this book on an individual basis. You might serve a cold appetizer plate, a heart-warming soup, or a crisp stir-fried vegetable as part of your regular meal, or practice with one of the simple, family-style one-pot meals. Wait to serve a multi-course Chinese meal when you have become familiar with the ingredients and techniques.

Variety is the goal you strive for when designing a Chinese meal for guests. As a rule of thumb, cook one dish per person plus soup and steamed rice. Fruit is the traditional dessert, but when you feel adventurous, check the index for a selection of Chinese desserts.

To achieve variety in the main part of the menu, select dishes that will provide contrasts in flavors, textures, and colors. Good Chinese cooking begins in the market, so adjust your menu or recipes to take advantage of each vegetable as it comes in season.

Make it easy for yourself. Choose dishes that call for different cooking techniques, such as one baked dish, one deep-fried dish, and one braised dish, and eliminate as much last minute cooking as possible. Often two dishes can cook at the same time, such as a braised meat and a steamed fish. Or you can cook a braised dish ahead of time and reheat it. Stir-fried dishes should be served immediately after cooking. Until you are more comfortable with Chinese cooking, include only one stir-fried dish in your menu unless you want to serve the meal in courses, rather than all at one time (family-style).

With menu in hand, here's a checklist to follow: read each recipe a second time so you completely understand the cooking technique; write a shopping list and purchase all ingredients, being sure to include those items you want to use for garnishes; organize a time schedule and decide in what order to cook each dish. While this planning may seem time-consuming at first, it is the key to presenting a well-timed and successful meal.

To make Chinese cooking a pleasure, take a tip from experienced chefs and do as much advance preparation as possible. Cut up vegetables, and slice and marinate meats ahead of time. Soak dried ingredients such as black mushrooms and wood ears. Combine sauce ingredients, leaving the cornstarch and water mixture in a separate bowl. If one ingredient (such as minced ginger) is used in several dishes, mince a small bowlful, then measure out the correct amount for each recipe. If you do this early in the day, cover and refrigerate the recipe components. Before you begin to cook, group each recipe's ingredients together on a separate tray. Keep basic seasonings such as soy sauce, sesame oil, dry sherry, vegetable oil, salt, and pepper near; you'll need those for more than one recipe. Set cooking pans, wok, utensils, steamer, and serving platters within easy reach.

Completely prepared to cook and serve a gourmet Chinese meal, all that is needed is for the lucky guests to arrive at your table. Just relax and remember this old Chinese saying: "Guest may wait for the food but the food never waits for the guest."

Remember this old Chinese saying: "Guests may wait for the food, but the food never waits for the guests."

SEA HARVEST IN A NEST

Makes: 4 to 6 servings
Cooking time: 20 minutes

 ¼ pound squid
6 to 8 medium-size raw shrimp,
  shelled and deveined
 ¼ pound sea scallops,
  halved horizontally

Marinade

 1 egg white, lightly beaten
 2 teaspoons each dry
  sherry and cornstarch
 ¼ teaspoon salt
  Dash of white pepper

 2 large potatoes (about
  1 pound total)
 ½ teaspoon salt

 12 fresh or canned quail eggs
  Vegetable oil for deep-
  frying

 1 clove garlic, minced
 1 teaspoon minced fresh
  ginger
 1 red bell pepper, seeded
  and thinly sliced
 1 can (8 ounces) sliced
  bamboo shoots, drained
 ½ zucchini, halved
  horizontally and thinly
  sliced
 ¼ cup chicken broth
 2 teaspoons dry sherry
 1 teaspoon sesame oil
 ½ teaspoon salt
  Dash of black pepper
 ½ teaspoon cornstarch
  mixed with 1 teaspoon
  water
 ¼ cup unsalted roasted
  cashews or almonds
 ½ head lettuce, shredded,
  for garnish

Preparation

To clean squid, separate head and tentacles from body. Cut off tentacles just above eyes, then remove and discard hard beak at center of tentacles; rinse tentacles and set aside. Discard remainder of head. Pull out stiff pen from body. Slit body open and rinse thoroughly. Peel off speckled membrane and rinse again. Lightly score inside of body in a small crisscross pattern; cut body into 1½- by 2-inch pieces.

In a large bowl, combine marinade ingredients. Add squid pieces, shrimp, and scallops; stir to coat. Set aside for 30 minutes.

Peel potatoes, then cut into 2-inch matchstick pieces. Set in a large bowl of water with ½ teaspoon salt until ready to cook.

If using fresh quail eggs, place in a small saucepan and pour in enough water to cover. Bring to a boil, then reduce heat, and simmer for 3 minutes. Rinse under cold running water. Remove and discard shells; set eggs aside.

Cooking

Drain potatoes thoroughly and pat dry with paper towels. Set wok in a ring stand and add oil to a depth of 2 inches. Place over medium-high heat until oil reaches about 360°F. Spread half the potatoes evenly over sides and bottom of a lightly oiled wire strainer. Press a second wire strainer of the same size down into the first to form a potato "nest". Holding strainers together, cook nest until evenly browned, carefully pouring oil over all sides with a ladle. Lift out, gently tapping nest to loosen it from strainers. Drain on paper towels. Repeat with remaining potatoes and set nests aside.

Reheat remaining oil in wok over medium heat until oil reaches about 325°F. Add squid pieces, shrimp, and scallops; blanch for 1 minute. Lift out and drain on paper towels.

Remove all but 2 tablespoons oil from wok.

Reheat oil over high heat until hot. Add garlic and ginger; cook, stirring, until fragrant. Add bell pepper, bamboo shoots, and zucchini; stir-fry for 1½ minutes. Add quail eggs, squid, shrimp, and scallops; cook and toss for 1 minute. Add broth, sherry, sesame oil, salt, black pepper, and cornstarch solution and cook, stirring, until mixture boils and thickens. Remove from heat. Add cashews and toss to mix. To serve, line a platter with shredded lettuce and arrange potato nests on top. Fill each nest with half the seafood mixture.

Pictured on page 54

SHRIMP-FILLED DELICACIES

Makes: 4 servings
Cooking time: 18 minutes

- 1 medium green bell pepper
- 2 medium tomatoes, cut in half
- 1 small cucumber, cut crosswise into 1½-inch sections

Filling

- ¾ pound medium-size raw shrimp, shelled and deveined
- 1 egg white
- 1 tablespoon cornstarch
- ½ teaspoon salt
- ¼ teaspoon each pepper and sesame oil

Braising Sauce

- ½ cup chicken broth
- 2 tablespoons each plum sauce and ketchup
- 1 tablespoon soy sauce
- 1 teaspoon sugar

  Cornstarch for coating
- 2 teaspoons vegetable oil

Preparation

Cut peppers into quarters and remove seeds. Scoop pulp from tomato halves. Scoop out center portion of each cucumber section with a melon baller (cucumber sections should be open at both ends). Set all vegetables aside.

In a food processor or blender, whirl filling ingredients into a smooth paste. Transfer filling to a bowl, cover, and refrigerate for 1 to 2 hours.

Combine braising sauce ingredients in a small bowl and set aside.

Stuff cucumber, tomato halves, and bell pepper quarters with filling. Lightly dust surfaces of all vegetables with cornstarch, shaking off excess.

Cooking

Place a wok or wide frying pan over medium-high heat until hot. Add oil, swirling to coat sides. Place stuffed vegetables in pan, filling side down. Cook vegetables for 1½ to 2 minutes on each side or until evenly browned.

Pour braising sauce over stuffed vegetables and bring to a boil. Reduce heat, cover, and simmer, stirring occasionally, for 10 to 12 minutes or until bell pepper is tender. Remove and arrange, filling side up, on a large serving platter. Serve hot.

(continued on page 56)

CLOCKWISE FROM RIGHT: Steamed Sea Bass (page 56);
black sesame seed rolls, Sweet Rice Balls (page 63), small
and large moon cakes, and sweet sesame balls; Sea Harvest
in a Nest (page 52); Twin Mushrooms (page 46);

(continued from page 53)

Tips

If fuzzy or bitter melons are available, you can cut them in the same way as the cucumber for a delicious alternative.

Bitter melon is also known as "foo-gwa". This marrow-like vegetable resembles a wrinkled cucumber. Quinine gives it the cool, bitter taste. Don't peel bitter melon, but scoop out the seeds and pulp prior to use. If you wish, you can parboil it in salted water for 3 minutes to reduce the bitterness, then stir-fry or stuff.

STEAMED SEA BASS

Makes: 4 servings
Cooking time: 18 minutes

    1 whole sea bass (about 2
      pounds), cleaned and
      scaled
    5 green onions (including
      tops)
    2 tablespoons 2-inch slivers
      fresh ginger
    3 tablespoons dark soy
      sauce
    2 teaspoons sesame oil
      Dash of white pepper
    3 tablespoons vegetable oil,
      heated

      Cilantro (Chinese parsley)
      sprigs, for garnish

Preparation

On each side of fish, make 3 or 4 diagonal slashes about 1 inch apart, cutting down to the bone each time. Place 2 of the green onions on the bottom of a heatproof dish, then lay fish on top. Sprinkle with half the slivered ginger.

Cut remaining green onions into 2-inch slivers and set aside.

Cooking

Place dish in a steamer or on a rack in a wok. Cover and steam over boiling water for 10 to 12 minutes or until fish turns opaque.

To serve, transfer fish to a large serving platter. Sprinkle soy sauce, sesame oil, and white pepper over fish. Top with slivered green onions. Pour heated oil over fish and garnish with cilantro sprigs. Serve immediately.

Tips

The cooking time may vary, depending on the thickness of the fish.

Substitute red snapper, rock cod, or carp for the sea bass, if desired.

If dark soy sauce is unavailable, use 3 tablespoons regular soy sauce.

Pictured on page 55

SALT-BAKED CHICKEN

Makes: 6 servings
Cooking time: 1½ hours

Filling

1 small onion, coarsely
  chopped
1 shallot, coarsely chopped
2 tablespoons soy sauce
1 tablespoon *each* minced
  fresh ginger and dry sherry
½ teaspoon *each* salt and
  Chinese five-spice

1 frying chicken (about
  3 pounds), cleaned
5 pounds rock salt

Preparation

Combine filling ingredients in a bowl. Pat chicken dry inside and out. Spoon filling into chicken body cavity, then close cavity with trussing needles. Cover and refrigerate overnight.

Pour salt into a deep ovenproof casserole dish (large enough to hold chicken). Bake in a 375°F oven for 20 minutes. Remove from oven and let salt cool to room temperature.

Cooking

Wrap chicken in a double layer of cheesecloth. Remove three-quarters of the cooled salt from casserole dish and set aside. Rearrange remaining salt to form a flat bed inside casserole dish. Place wrapped chicken, breast side up, on salt bed, then cover chicken with reserved salt. Cover casserole dish and bake in a 375°F oven for 1¼ hours or until meat near thighbone is no longer pink when slashed.

Carefully lift chicken from casserole dish and place on a cutting board. Remove cheesecloth, brushing off salt particles. Cut chicken into serving-size pieces and arrange on a serving platter. Serve hot or cold.

Tips

Rock salt is a slow heat conductor; once it absorbs heat, it maintains a uniform temperature that cooks the chicken evenly.

Rock salt can be used more than once.

SIZZLING BLACK BEAN CHICKEN

Makes: 4 servings
Cooking time: 5 minutes

Marinade

2 tablespoons dry sherry
1 tablespoon soy sauce
2 teaspoons sesame oil

2 whole chicken breasts, skinned, boned, and cut into ¾-inch cubes

¼ cup vegetable oil
2 cloves garlic, minced
2 teaspoons minced fresh ginger
3 shallots, finely chopped
1 green onion (including top), finely chopped
2 to 3 tablespoons fermented black beans
6 dried whole red chili peppers (optional)
½ teaspoon crushed red pepper
¾ cup chicken broth
1 teaspoon soy sauce
½ teaspoon sugar
¾ teaspoon cornstarch mixed with 1 ½ teaspoons water

Preparation

Combine marinade ingredients in a large bowl. Add chicken; stir to coat. Set aside for 30 minutes.

Cooking

Place wok or wide frying pan over high heat until hot. Add 2 tablespoons of the oil, swirling to coat sides. Add chicken; stir-fry for about 3 minutes or until opaque. Remove chicken and set aside.

Keep warm. Add remaining 2 tablespoons oil to wok. When oil is hot, add garlic, ginger, shallots, and green onion; cook, stirring, for 1 minute. Add black beans, whole chili peppers, crushed red peppers, broth, soy sauce, and sugar; stir-fry for 30 seconds. Add cornstarch solution and cook, stirring, until mixture boils and thickens.

To serve, place chicken on a hot cast iron plate then pour hot black bean sauce over chicken. Serve immediately while still sizzling.

Tips

Caution: When sauce is poured over, chicken will spatter vigorously in the hot plate. Be careful when serving—don't lean over the plate or bring your face too close to the food.

This restaurant specialty is served on a cast iron plate. If you don't have a cast-iron plate, use a cast iron frying pan.

Martin Yan, The Chinese Chef

EIGHT PRECIOUS DUCK

Makes: 6 to 8 servings
Cooking time: 2 to 2½ hours

1 duckling (4 to 5 pounds),
cleaned

Marinade

2 tablespoons soy sauce
1 tablespoon honey
1 teaspoon sesame oil

Stuffing

1 cup glutinous rice
2 tablespoons dried shrimp
4 dried black mushrooms
¼ cup dried lotus seeds
(optional)
1 tablespoon sugar
(optional; needed only if
lotus seeds are used)
2 teaspoons vegetable oil
2 cloves garlic, minced
½ Chinese sausage (1
ounce), thinly sliced
2 green onions (including
tops), minced
¼ cup matchstick pieces
bamboo shoots
2 tablespoons soy sauce
1 tablespoon hoisin sauce
2 teaspoons dry sherry
1 teaspoon sesame oil

Preparation

Cut off and discard excess neck skin from duck. Remove and discard fat from around body cavity; prick duck all over with a bamboo skewer. Combine marinade ingredients in a large bowl. Add duck; turn to coat. Cover and refrigerate for at least 2 to 3 hours or overnight.

Soak rice in enough warm water to cover for 1 hour; drain and set aside. Soak shrimp in enough warm water to cover for 30 minutes; drain. In a separate bowl, soak mushrooms in enough warm water to cover for 30 minutes; drain. Cut off and discard mushroom stems; coarsely chop caps. Set mushrooms and shrimp aside.

If using lotus seeds, bring ¾ cup water to a boil in a small saucepan. Add lotus seeds and sugar; stir until sugar is dissolved. Reduce heat, cover and simmer, stirring occasionally, for about 35 minutes or until seeds are tender to bite. Drain and set aside.

Line the bottom of a steamer with a damp cheesecloth. Place soaked rice on cheesecloth. Cover and steam over boiling water for 30 minutes. Lift out and set aside.

Cooking

Place wok or wide frying pan over high heat until hot. Add oil, swirling to coat sides. Add garlic; cook, stirring, until fragrant. Add shrimp, mushrooms, Chinese sausage, and green onions; stir-fry for 1 minute. Add lotus seeds, bamboo shoots, soy sauce, hoisin sauce, sherry, and sesame oil; mix well. Remove from heat and add rice; toss to mix well.

Lift out duck from marinade and drain. Spoon stuffing into duck body cavity, then close with trussing needles. Place duck, breast side up, on a rack over a foil-lined baking pan. Roast in a 350°F oven for about 1½ hours or until juices run clear when thigh is pierced. Carefully turn duck a few times during roasting.

(continued on next page)

(continued from previous page)

Spoon out stuffing and mound in center of a large platter. Cut duck into large serving-size pieces and place on top of stuffing, arranging them in the shape of a whole duck.

Tips

Dried shrimp are shelled, salted, and dried tiny shrimp that have a strong flavor that enhances dishes and soup. Soak in enough warm water to cover for 30 minutes before using.

Pictured on page 35

CURRIED RICE STICK NOODLES

Makes: 4 servings
Cooking time: 8 minutes

- 6 dried black mushrooms
- 8 cups water
- 1 package (about 7 ounces) rice stick noodles, broken in half
- ½ cup cold water
- 5 tablespoons vegetable oil
- 2 eggs, lightly beaten
- 1 shallot, thinly sliced
- ½ small onion, thinly sliced
- 2 green onions (including tops), cut diagonally into 2-inch pieces
- 2 ounces Chinese BBQ Pork (page 38), cut into matchstick pieces
- 2 ounces small cooked shrimp
- 1 cup bean sprouts
- 3 tablespoons *each* soy sauce and chicken broth
- 4 teaspoons curry powder
- 2 teaspoons sesame oil
- ½ teaspoon salt
- ¼ teaspoon turmeric
  Dash of Chinese five-spice

Preparation

Soak mushrooms in enough warm water to cover for 30 minutes; drain. Cut off and discard stems; thinly slice caps. Set aside.

Cooking

Bring 8 cups water to a boil in a large pot. Add rice stick noodles, stirring to separate strands. When water returns to a boil, add ½ cup cold water. Return to a boil again and cook, stirring occasionally, for about 2 minutes or until noodles are tender to bite. Pour into a colander, rinse under cold running water and drain well. Set aside.

Place a wok or wide frying pan over medium-high heat until hot. Add 1 tablespoon of the vegetable oil, swirling to coat sides. Pour in eggs, tilting wok to coat bottom evenly. Cook just until eggs are set and feel dry on top. Remove eggs from wok and let cool slightly. Cut into thin 1-inch-long strips. Set aside.

Place clean wok over medium-high heat until hot. Add remaining 4 tablespoons oil, swirling to coat sides. Add shallot, sliced onion, and green onions; stir-fry for about 1 minute or until onions are limp. Add mushrooms, pork, shrimp, and bean sprouts; stir-fry for 1 minute.

Reduce heat to medium. Stir in cooked noodles, tossing to mix well. Add soy sauce, broth, curry powder, sesame oil, salt, turmeric, and five-spice;

Martin Yan, The Chinese Chef

toss to mix well. Sprinkle top with egg strips. Serve immediately.

Tips

Use rice stick noodles in soups, and in stir-fried or deep-fried dishes. If stir-frying, don't overcook the noodles or they will break.

ALMOND TEA

Makes: 8 servings
Cooking time: 15 minutes

Almond Paste

¼ cup long-grain rice
6 ounces blanched almonds
1½ cups water

6 cups water
1¼ cups sugar
½ cup evaporated milk or
    half-and-half
¼ teaspoon almond extract

Preparation

Soak rice in enough water to cover for at least 2 hours or overnight; drain. In a food processor or blender, whirl rice, almonds, and 1 ½ cups water into a smooth paste. Transfer paste to a large pot.

Cooking

Add 6 cups water and sugar to almond paste. Bring to a boil, stirring constantly, until sugar is dissolved. Reduce heat and simmer, uncovered, for 10 minutes. Set a fine strainer lined with a double layer of damp cheesecloth over a deep bowl. Pour soup through strainer into bowl, then gather cheesecloth and squeeze firmly to extract all remaining liquid.

Return liquid to pot; stir in evaporated milk and heat just to simmering. Stir in almond extract. Serve hot in individual soup bowls. Or, cover and refrigerate until well chilled and serve cold.

Tips

If you wish, you may substitute walnuts, peanuts or sesame seeds for the almonds. Follow the same procedure.

SWEET WATER CHESTNUT SOUP

Makes: 8 to 10 servings
Cooking time: 15 minutes

- ½ cup peeled green mung beans
- 11 cups water
- 2 cans (8 ounces *each*) sliced water chestnuts, drained and coarsely chopped
- ¾ cup sugar
- 1 can (8 ounces) crushed pineapple, drained
- 1 tablespoon cornstarch mixed with 2 tablespoons water
- ¼ cup water chestnut powder mixed with ½ cup water
- Grated lemon peel, for garnish

Preparation

Place beans in a colander and rinse briefly under cold running water. Then soak beans in enough water to cover for 30 minutes; drain.

Cooking

In a large pot, bring beans and 6 cups of the water to a boil. Reduce heat and simmer for 8 to 10 minutes. Drain well.

In another large pot, bring remaining 5 cups water to a boil. Reduce heat to medium and stir in beans and water chestnuts; blend well. Stir in sugar and pineapple; cook, stirring, until heated through. Add cornstarch solution and water chestnut powder solution. Cook, stirring constantly, until soup thickens slightly. Serve in individual soup bowls. Garnish with grated lemon peel.

Tips

Peeled green mung beans are available only in Chinese grocery stores. They look like small yellow split peas.

When adding water chestnut powder to hot liquid, be sure to stir quickly and constantly—it thickens almost instantly. Water chestnut powder is available only in Chinese grocery stores.

Martin Yan, The Chinese Chef

SWEET RICE BALLS

Makes: 12 rice balls
Cooking time: 10 minutes

Filling

2 tablespoons sesame seeds

¼ cup finely chopped
   unsalted roasted peanuts

3 tablespoons sugar

Dough

3 cups glutinous rice flour

⅔ cup boiling water

½ cup plus 2 tablespoons
   cold water

12 wax paper squares, *each*
   4- by 4-inches

Finely shredded
sweetened coconut

Preparation

In a wide frying pan, toast sesame seeds over medium heat for about 5 minutes or until golden brown, shaking pan frequently. Place in a small bowl and stir in remaining filling ingredients. Set aside.

Measure rice flour in a medium-size bowl. Make a well in the center of flour and pour boiling water into well, stirring with chopsticks or a fork until dough is evenly moistened. Add cold water and stir until dough forms a ball.

On a lightly floured surface, knead dough for about 5 minutes or until smooth and shiny. Cover with a damp cloth and let rest for 10 minutes. Roll dough into a 12-inch-long cylinder. Cut cylinder crosswise into 1-inch pieces.

To shape each dumpling, flatten one piece of dough with a rolling pin to make a ¼-inch-thick circle, keeping remaining dough covered to prevent drying. Place 1½ teaspoons of filling in center of circle. Gather and pinch edges together at the top to seal securely. Roll carefully between your palms to form a round ball. Place on a square of wax paper. Cover filled dumplings with a damp cloth while filling remaining dumplings.

Cooking

Line the bottom of a steamer with a small damp towel. Arrange dumplings, without crowding, on cloth. Cover and steam over boiling water for 10 minutes. Remove dumplings and sprinkle evenly with coconut. Serve immediately.

Tips
These steamed sweet balls have a dense, sticky texture similar to that of Japanese rice cakes (mochi).

Pictured on page 54

Canton

In southern China since the 10th century, teahouses have been an important place for family, friends, and business associates to meet and partake of dim sum.

Dim sum literally means point *(dim)* to the heart *(sum)* or "touches the heart" because you point to and choose the dish you want. There is no menu. The dozens of small morsels, sweet-filled pastries, and breads have been popular fare in Chinatowns throughout North America and other parts of the world since their introduction in the 1800s.

If you have never experienced the pleasures of a dim sum lunch, it is better to go the first time with someone who is familiar with the selections. Dim sum comes three ways: fried dumplings, steamed buns or dumplings, and those prepared by stir-frying or braising. There are also sweet pastries filled with sweetened black, red, or lotus bean paste. Dim sum is served from carts filled with plates and little bamboo steamers, each holding three pastries (three is considered a lucky number by Chinese). Choose as many different dishes as you wish; at the end of the meal, the bill is calculated by the number of empty dishes on the table.

Nobody really knows the origin of dim sum. It started out as special gifts to exchange with friends during festive occasions, such as Chinese New Year, Dragon Boat Festival, and August Moon. It was the Cantonese, during the Sung dynasty, who began preparing dim sum for the teahouses. These tidbits became so popular that Cantonese teahouses throughout China built reputations around a core of dim sum dishes that have become classics.

Today, chefs are creating new dim sum dishes because of the vast array of ingredients and kitchen tools available to them. When going to Chinatown for dim sum, remember that it is generally served between 9 A.M. and 2 P.M.

"Yum Cha" is the Chinese invitation to "go eat dim sum or have a cup of tea."

Martin Yan, The Chinese Chef

CRISPY NUT POCKETS

Makes: 24 pockets
Cooking time: 7 minutes

Filling

¼ pound preserved pitted
  dates
¼ cup *each* unsalted roasted
  peanuts and honey
4 teaspoons finely chopped
  candied ginger

24 pot sticker wrappers
1 egg white, lightly beaten

Vegetable oil for deep-
  frying

Preparation

Combine filling ingredients in a bowl; mix well.
Set aside.

To fill dumplings, place 1 heaping teaspoon of
filling into center of each wrapper, keeping
remaining wrappers covered to prevent drying.
Lightly brush edges of wrapper with egg white.
Fold circle in half over filling to form a semi-circle,
pressing edges to seal. Cover filled wrappers with a
damp cloth while filling remaining wrappers.

Cooking

Set wok in a ring stand and add oil to a depth of
2 inches. Place over medium-high heat until oil
reaches about 375°F. Cook pockets, a few at a time,
for about 1 to 1½ minutes or until golden brown,
turning occasionally. Lift out and drain on paper
towels. Keep warm in a 200°F oven while cooking
remaining pockets. Serve immediately.

SZECHUAN & HUNAN

Regional dishes from Szechuan and Hunan offer an intriguing, often surprising combination of flavors: hot, sour, sweet, and salty.

CLOKWISE FROM RIGHT: Smoke Tea Duck (page 88); Seafood Medley over Sizzling Rice (page 81); Szechuan Omelet Soup (page 74); and Mu Shu Pork (page 75).

Szechuan/Hunan

"Food from Szechuan and Hunan is unique. Don't be timid when tasting these spicy specialties."

These two hot, humid provinces are well inland. Hunan is immediately north of Guangdong, my home province, and Sichuan (Szechuan) lies to the northwest of Hunan. Although the cuisines of these two regions are grouped together by geography, both provinces being relatively central, they remain distinctly individual in character.

Although similar in climate, these two provinces have very different topographies. Sichuan is a harsh region with rocky crags and deep valleys; Hunan has gentler rolling hills with fertile soil and generous rainfall.

Sichuan cuisine has enjoyed increasing popularity over the years for two interesting reasons. When fleeing invading Japanese forces in 1937, the Nationalist government moved to Sichuan. After the war, they returned to power, introducing the cuisine as far east as Taiwan. Since then, Sichuan food has taken the tastebuds of the world by storm.

A second reason for the cuisine's popularity is its intriguing combinations of hot, sour, sweet, and salty tastes, a trait shared by the foods of neighboring Hunan. This quality has much to do with the heavy use of aromatic peppercorns and hot chilis.

Sichuan province has limited resources, and thus its cuisine is often simple and straightforward. Some commonly found ingredients in Sichuan recipes are pork, poultry, and soybean products.

Hunan province, on the other hand, boasts an abundance of foods, including an array of vegetables that Sichuan lacks. One interesting characteristic of Hunan cuisine is that many of the meats in the region's recipes are marinated or preserved. On the whole, Hunan cuisine tends to be richer than that of neighboring Sichuan.

Martin Yan, The Chinese Chef

A natural preservative, hot chili is an important feature when one prepares food in a hot, humid climate without refrigeration. When used judiciously, chilis should not burn the mouth. Ideally, they will sensitize the palate, allowing the nuances of seasoning combinations —notably sweet, sour, and salty tastes—to come forth.

The spicy specialties of Hunan and Sichuan cuisines can be as hot or as mild as your palate dictates, and are always uniquely flavorful. So, don't be shy about exploring the dynamic cuisine of inland China.

SUGGESTED MENUS

Szechuan Omelet Soup
Fish with Spicy Tomato Sauce
Smoke Tea Duck
Fruit & Snow Mushrooms

Szechuan Cucumber Salad
Seafood Medley over Sizzling Rice
Five Fragrant Beef
Peanut-Filled Snow Puffs

Cheng Du Dumplings with Peanut Sauce
Szechuan Mustard Green with Tomato
Kung Pao Shrimp
Zha Jiang Mein

SZECHUAN CUCUMBER SALAD

Makes: 4 servings
Cooking time: 3 minutes

  1 large English cucumber
  1 teaspoon salt

Dressing

  3 cloves garlic, minced
  2 teaspoons ground toasted
     Szechuan peppercorns
  2 tablespoons rice vinegar
  2 teaspoons *each* sesame oil
     and sugar
  ¾ teaspoons chili oil

  3 tablespoons vegetable oil

Preparation

Cut cucumber in half lengthwise, then cut each half crosswise into ¾-inch sections. To make cucumber fans, score each cucumber section, making cuts close together and cutting to within ¼ inch of edge each time. Sprinkle scored pieces with salt. Let stand for at least 30 minutes, then rinse cucumber pieces and pat dry with paper towels. Gently press each cucumber piece so slices spread out to form a fan. Transfer to a serving bowl and set aside.

Cooking

Heat a small saucepan over medium heat until hot. Add oil, swirling to coat sides. Add garlic and ground peppercorns; cook, stirring, until fragrant. Remove from pan; let cool. Stir in rice vinegar, sesame oil, sugar, and chili oil until blended.

Pour dressing over cucumber fans; mix well. Serve at room temperature or refrigerate and serve cold.

Pictured on page 87

Martin Yan, The Chinese Chef

SPICY SHRIMP SALAD

Makes: 4 to 6 servings
Cooking time: 3 minutes

- 4 cups water
- 2 ounces bean thread noodles, broken in half
- ½ cup cold water
- 1 teaspoon sesame oil
- ½ Chinese turnip, cut into matchstick pieces
- 1 large cucumber, peeled, seeded, and cut into matchstick pieces
- 1 small carrot, cut into matchstick pieces
- ¼ pound small cooked shrimp
- 1 green onion (including top), cut diagonally into 2-inch pieces

Dressing

- 2 tablespoons vegetable oil
- 2 cloves garlic, minced
- 3 tablespoons *each* chicken broth and rice vinegar
- 3 tablespoons chunky peanut butter or sesame seed paste
- 2 tablespoons *each* soy sauce and slivered pickled ginger (optional)
- 1 tablespoon sesame oil
- 1½ teaspoons sugar
- ¾ teaspoon chili oil
- Dash of black pepper

Cooking

In a medium-size saucepan, bring 4 cups of the water to a boil. Add noodles, stirring to separate strands. When water returns to a boil, add ½ cup cold water. Return to a boil again and cook, stirring occasionally, for about 2 minutes or until noodles are tender to bite. Pour into a colander, rinse under cold running water, and drain well. Toss with sesame oil and set aside.

Blanch turnip in a small saucepan of boiling water for 1 minute. Rinse under cold running water and drain; let cool.

In a serving bowl, combine noodles, turnip, cucumber, carrot, shrimp, and green onion; toss well. Set aside.

Heat a small saucepan over medium-high heat until hot. Add oil, swirling to coat sides. Add garlic; cook, stirring, until fragrant. Stir in remaining dressing ingredients until well blended. Bring to a boil and cook for 30 seconds. Remove from heat and let cool.

Pour dressing over salad; toss to coat well. Cover and refrigerate until well chilled. Serve cold.

CURRIED BEEF TURNOVERS

Makes: 15 dumplings
Cooking time: 25 minutes

Sauce

2½ teaspoons curry powder
2 teaspoons soy sauce
1 teaspoon Szechuan chili paste
½ teaspoon sugar
¼ teaspoon Chinese five-spice
1 teaspoon cornstarch mixed with 2 teaspoons water

Dough

2⅔ cups all-purpose flour
1 cup solid vegetable shortening
½ teaspoon salt
½ cup water

1 tablespoon vegetable oil
¼ pound ground lean beef
¼ cup finely chopped onion
1 green onion (including top), minced

1 egg yolk, beaten

Preparation

Combine sauce ingredients in a small bowl; mix well. Set aside. Measure flour into a medium-size bowl; cut shortening into flour until crumbly. Gradually add salt and water and knead to make a smooth dough. On a lightly floured surface, roll dough into a 15-inch-long cylinder. Cut crosswise into 1-inch pieces; shape each piece into a ball. Cover with a damp cloth and set aside.

Cooking

Place a wok or a wide frying pan over high heat until hot. Add oil, swirling to coat sides. Add beef, chopped onion, and green onion; stir-fry for 1½ to 2 minutes or until beef is browned. Add sauce; cook, stirring, until sauce boils and thickens slightly. Remove from heat and let cool to room temperature.

To shape each dumpling, flatten one ball of dough with a rolling pin to make a 3- to 3½-inch circle, keeping remaining dough covered to prevent drying. Place 2 teaspoons of curry filling in center of each circle. Lightly moisten edges of dough with water. Fold dough in half over filling, pressing edges together to form a semicircle. Then press around edges with the tines of a fork. Brush top of dumpling lightly with beaten egg yolk. Place on an ungreased baking sheet. Cover filled dumplings with a damp cloth while shaping remaining dumplings.

Bake in a 450°F oven for 15 to 20 minutes or until lightly browned. Serve hot.

Martin Yan, The Chinese Chef

CHENG DU DUMPLINGS WITH PEANUT SAUCE

Makes: 30 dumplings
Cooking time: 12 minutes

Filling

- ½ pound boneless lean pork, minced
- ¼ pound medium-size raw shrimp, shelled, deveined, and minced
- 3 cups finely shredded Chinese (napa) cabbage
- 2 tablespoons soy sauce
- 1 green onion (including top), minced
- 1 tablespoon each dry sherry and cornstarch
- 2 teaspoons each minced fresh ginger and sesame oil
- ½ teaspoon sugar
- ¼ teaspoon salt

Dipping Sauce

- 1 clove garlic, minced
- ¼ cup chunky peanut butter
- 3 tablespoons chicken broth
- 2 tablespoons soy sauce
- 2 teaspoons finely chopped cilantro (Chinese parsley) leaves (optional)
- 2 teaspoons sesame oil
- 1 green onion (white part only), minced

Dough

- 3 cups all-purpose flour
- 1⅓ cups boiling water

- 12 cups water
- 1 cup cold water

Preparation

Combine filling ingredients in a bowl; mix well and set aside.

In another bowl, combine dipping sauce ingredients until well blended. Set aside.

Measure flour into a bowl. Mix in boiling water, stirring with chopsticks or a fork until dough is evenly moistened.

On a lightly floured surface, knead dough until smooth. Cover and let rest for about 30 minutes. Divide dough in half. Roll each half into a 15-inch-long cylinder. Cut each cylinder crosswise into 1-inch pieces; shape each piece into a ball.

To shape each dumpling, flatten one ball of dough with a rolling pin to make a 3- to 3½-inch circle, keeping remaining dough covered to prevent drying. Place 1 heaping teaspoon of filling in center of each circle. Fold circle in half over filling to form a semicircle. Starting at one end, pinch curved edges together; make 4 to 5 pleats along the edge facing you, pressing edges to seal securely. Cover filled dumplings with a damp cloth while shaping remaining dumplings.

Cooking

In a large pot, bring 12 cups water to a boil. Add half the dumplings, without crowding, stirring to separate. When water returns to a boil, add ½ cup of the cold water. Return to a boil again and cook, stirring, until dumplings start to float. Lift out dumplings with a wire strainer and place in a heatproof serving dish. Keep warm in a 200°F oven while cooking remaining dumplings. Serve dumplings hot with dipping sauce.

Pictured on page 86

SZECHUAN OMELET SOUP

Makes: 6 servings
Cooking time: 35 minutes

- 1 tablespoon dried shrimp
- 2 ounces ground lean pork or beef
- 1 tablespoon minced Szechuan preserved vegetables
- 2 teaspoons soy sauce
- 1 teaspoon *each* sesame oil and cornstarch
  About 4 tablespoons vegetable oil
- ¼ cup chopped bamboo shoots
- 2 green onions (including tops), minced
- 3 eggs, lightly beaten
- ¼ teaspoon salt
- 5 cups Basic Chicken Broth (page 106)
- 2 cups shredded small green leaves (spinach, watercress, or bok choy)

Preparation

Soak shrimp in enough warm water to cover for 30 minutes; drain. Coarsely chop and set aside.

Combine pork, preserved vegetables, soy sauce, sesame oil, and cornstarch; mix well. Set aside for 15 minutes.

Cooking

Place a wok or wide frying pan over medium-high heat until hot. Add 2 teaspoons of the oil, swirling to coat sides. Add shrimp, pork mixture, bamboo shoots, and green onions; stir-fry for 2 minutes or until meat is lightly browned. Remove and set aside.

Beat eggs with salt. Place a small frying pan with a nonstick finish over medium heat until hot. Add 1 teaspoon of the oil, swirling to coat sides. Pour in about 1 tablespoon of the eggs. Immediately tilt pan in all directions so egg spreads to form a thin 3-inch circle. Then place 1½ teaspoons of filling in center of each omelet.

When egg is set on the bottom but still liquid on top, fold circle in half over filling and press edges lightly with a spatula to seal. Remove omelet from pan and set aside. Cook remaining omelets.

In a large pot, bring broth to a boil. Add green leaves; reduce heat and simmer, uncovered, for 1 minute. Add omelets and continue to simmer for 1 more minute. Spoon 1 or 2 omelets and part of the greens into individual serving bowls. Serve hot.

Tips

Omelets can be prepared a day ahead and refrigerated.

Pictured on page 66

Martin Yan, The Chinese Chef

MU SHU PORK

Makes: 6 to 8 servings
Cooking time: 10 minutes

> 2 ounces tiger lily buds
> 4 to 6 cloud ears
> 4 dried black mushrooms

Filling

> 2½ tablespoons vegetable oil
> 2 eggs, lightly beaten
> 1 clove garlic, minced
> ½ teaspoon minced fresh ginger
> ½ pound boneless lean pork, cut into matchstick pieces
> 4 cups finely shredded cabbage (about ½ pound)
> 1 small carrot, cut into 1-inch slivers
> 2 green onions (including tops), cut into 1-inch slivers
> ½ cup chicken broth
> 2 tablespoons soy sauce
> 1 tablespoon dry sherry
> 1 teaspoon sesame oil
> 1½ teaspoons cornstarch mixed with 1 tablespoon water
>
> About 16 Mandarin Pancakes (page *124*)
> ¼ cup hoisin sauce

Preparation

Soak tiger lily buds, cloud ears, and mushrooms *separately* in enough warm water to cover for 30 minutes; drain. Cut off hard knobby ends of lily buds and tie each bud into a knot. Cut off and discard mushroom stems; thinly slice caps. Set lily buds, cloud ears, and mushrooms aside.

Place a wide frying pan with a nonstick finish over medium-high heat until hot. Add 1½ teaspoons of the oil, swirling to coat sides. Pour in half the eggs, tilting pan to coat bottom evenly. Cook just until eggs are set and feel dry on top. Remove from pan and let cool slightly while cooking remaining eggs. Cut into thin 1-inch-long strips and set aside.

Cooking

Place a wok or wide frying pan over high heat until hot. Add remaining 2 tablespoons oil, swirling to coat sides. Add garlic and ginger; cook, stirring, until fragrant. Add pork; stir-fry for about 2 minutes or until lightly browned. Add lily buds, cloud ears, mushrooms, cabbage, carrot, green onions, and broth. Cook and toss for 2 minutes. Stir in soy sauce, sherry, and sesame oil; mix well. Add cornstarch solution and cook, stirring, until sauce boils and thickens. Toss in egg strips and mix well.

Meanwhile, place pancakes in a heatproof dish. Set dish in a steamer or on a rack in a wok. Cover and steam over boiling water for 5 minutes or until heated through.

To serve, spread a small amount of hoisin sauce on each pancake. Place about 3 tablespoons of meat-vegetable mixture in center of pancake. Wrap like a burrito. Serve warm.

Tips

Cloud ears and wood ears, also known as tree mushrooms, are found in Chinese markets. In China, an ear refers to a fungus which is crunchy in texture. Cloud ears, packaged in plastic bags, are small, brownish-black pieces that are slightly transparent. Wood ears, packaged in larger plastic bags, are large, brownish-black ear-shaped pieces with light color undersides.

Pictured on page 66

FIVE-FRAGRANT BEEF

Makes: 4 to 6 servings
Cooking time: 1 ¾ hours

2 pounds boneless beef chuck

Sauce

4 thin slices fresh ginger, each 1 by 2 inches
3 green onions (including tops), cut in half
2 whole star anise
4 cups water
⅓ cup soy sauce
¼ cup dry sherry or Shao Hsing wine
3 tablespoons dark soy sauce
1 tablespoon packed brown sugar
1 teaspoon Chinese five-spice
½ teaspoon ground toasted Szechuan peppercorns

Preparation

Trim and discard excess fat from beef. Combine sauce ingredients in a heavy large pot. Add beef; turn to coat.

Cooking

Bring beef and sauce to a boil. Reduce heat, cover, and simmer for about 1 ¾ hours or until beef is tender when pierced, turning beef occasionally.

Remove beef; thinly slice and arrange on a serving platter. Serve hot or cold.

Tips

If desired, strain sauce and use in other stewed dishes. Or, to serve meat with sauce, lightly thicken ¾ cup of the strained sauce with a cornstarch solution. Pour sauce over sliced meat.

Martin Yan, The Chinese Chef

SZECHUAN PRESERVED VEGETABLES WITH TOMATO

Makes: 4 servings
Cooking time: 12 minutes

1 package (about one pound) firm tofu (bean curd), drained

Sauce

2 tablespoons ketchup

1 tablespoon *each* dry sherry and soy sauce

¾ teaspoon sugar

Vegetable oil for deep-frying

1 ounce Szechuan preserved vegetables, cut into 2-inch matchstick pieces

2 green onions (including tops), cut diagonally into 2-inch pieces

2 tomatoes, peeled and cut into 8 wedges

Hot cooked rice

Preparation

Cut tofu in half horizontally to make two 1-inch-thick cakes. Cut each cake into quarters, then cut again diagonally to form a total of 16 triangles. Drain tofu triangles on paper towels and set aside.

Combine sauce ingredients in a bowl and set aside.

Cooking

Set wok in a ring stand and add oil to a depth of 1½ to 2 inches. Place over high heat until oil reaches about 375°F. Add tofu triangles, half at a time, and deep-fry for about 2 minutes or until triangles start to float, turning occasionally. Lift out and drain on paper towels. Cook remaining triangles.

Remove all but 2 tablespoons oil from wok. Reheat wok over high heat until hot. Add preserved vegetables and green onions; stir-fry for 1 minute. Add tofu and tomatoes; cook and stir for 1 minute. Add sauce and cook, stirring, for 2 to 3 minutes or until tofu is heated through. Transfer to a serving dish. Serve hot with rice.

VEGETARIAN STIR-FRY

Makes: 4 servings
Cooking time: 10 minutes

Sauce

   2 teaspoons sesame seeds
   ⅔ cup chicken or vegetarian broth
   2 tablespoons soy sauce
   ½ teaspoon sugar
   2 teaspoons cornstarch mixed with 1 tablespoon water

   6 to 8 dried black mushrooms
   1 small zucchini
   2 tablespoons vegetable oil
   2 teaspoons minced fresh ginger
   2 cups small broccoli flowerettes
   3 green onions (white parts only) cut diagonally into 2-inch pieces
   1 can (15 ounces) straw mushrooms, drained
   1 can (15 ounces) baby corn, drained
   ½ cup unsalted roasted peanuts or cashews

Preparation

In a wide frying pan, toast sesame seeds over medium heat for about 5 minutes or until golden brown, shaking pan frequently. Place sesame seeds in a bowl and add all remaining sauce ingredients except cornstarch solution; blend well. Set aside.

Soak mushrooms in enough warm water to cover for 30 minutes; drain. Cut off and discard stems; thinly slice caps. Set aside.

Slice zucchini in half horizontally then cut each half diagonally into ¼-inch-thick pieces; set aside.

Cooking

Place a wok or wide frying pan over high heat until hot. Add oil, swirling to coat sides. Add ginger; cook, stirring, until fragrant. Add mushrooms, broccoli, and green onions; stir-fry for 1 minute. Add straw mushrooms and sauce; cook and toss for 2 minutes. Add baby corn and zucchini; cover and cook for 2 to 3 minutes or until vegetables are crisp-tender, stirring occasionally. Add cornstarch solution and cook, stirring, until sauce boils and thickens slightly. Transfer to a serving dish. Sprinkle with nuts and serve hot.

Martin Yan, The Chinese Chef

The soybean is often called "the cow of China" because it is high in protein and because many high-protein, low-fat, essential products that are made from it.

Familiar to most of us is soy sauce, the multi-purpose flavoring sauce that has been an important component of Oriental cookery, as far back as the Han dynasty (206 B.C.–A.D. 220). There are two types of soy sauce: dark (thick) and light (thin). Dark soy sauce has a heavier consistency and is somewhat sweeter. Its dark color imparts a reddish-brown hue to the foods cooked in it, so it is used in "red-cooked" dishes. Light soy is an all-purpose soy sauce often used in marinades and in stir-fried dishes.

Tofu (fresh bean curd), the white custard-like product used extensively in Chinese as well as other Oriental cuisines, also has its humble beginnings in the soybean. Look for fresh tofu, soft or firm, in the produce section of most supermarkets, packed in water in plastic tubs. Store tofu in the refrigerator. Rinse after opening, cover any leftover tofu with cold water and refrigerate up to three days, changing water daily.

Another product, deep-fried bean curd, is available in the form of small pouches (often called puffs) and cubes.

Dried bean curd sheets or sticks are an important part of the Chinese vegetarian diet. They are made flexible by soaking briefly before using. Bean curd sheets or sticks can be stored in a cool dry place for 3 to 4 months.

Fermented bean curd comes in two versions, red and white. Pungent in flavor, both types are used in small quantities to give flavor to many family-style dishes. Fermented bean curd is packed in jars and is sold in Oriental markets.

"One tiny bean... its versatility affords Chinese cooking with such a range of flavors."

VEGETARIAN TOFU CASSEROLE

Makes: 4 servings
Cooking time: 15 minutes

- 6 dried black mushrooms
- 2 ounces bean thread noodles
- 4 cloud ears
- 24 tiger lily buds

Sauce

- 1½ cups chicken or vegetarian broth
- 2 tablespoons dry sherry
- 1 tablespoon soy sauce
- 1½ teaspoons sesame oil

- 2 tablespoons vegetable oil
- 2 cloves garlic, minced
- 2 tablespoons fermented red bean curd, mashed
- 8 ounces pressed bean curd, cut into thin slices
- 1 large carrot, cut into 2-inch matchstick pieces

Preparation

Soak mushrooms, noodles, cloud ears, and tiger lily buds *separately* in enough warm water to cover for 30 minutes; drain. Cut off and discard mushroom stems; thinly slice caps. Cut off hard knobby ends of lily buds and tie each bud into a knot. Set mushrooms, noodles, cloud ears, and lily buds aside.

Combine sauce ingredients in a bowl and set aside.

Cooking

Heat a wok or wide frying pan over high heat until hot. Add oil, swirling to coat sides. Add garlic; cook, stirring, until fragrant. Add mushrooms, noodles, cloud ears, lily buds, red bean curd, pressed bean curd, and carrot; cook and toss for 1 minute. Stir in sauce and bring to a boil. Reduce heat, cover, and cook for 10 minutes or until noodles absorb most of the liquid, stirring occasionally. Transfer to a serving bowl and serve hot.

Martin Yan, The Chinese Chef

SEAFOOD MEDLEY OVER SIZZLING RICE

Makes: 4 servings
Cooking time: 8 minutes

4 dried black mushrooms

Sauce

1 ½ cups chicken broth

2 tablespoons soy sauce

1 teaspoon *each* sesame oil
and chili oil

½ teaspoon sugar

¼ teaspoon salt
Dash of black pepper

2 tablespoons vegetable oil

¼ pound boneless lean pork,
cut into thin 1-by 2-inch
pieces

½ pound medium-size raw
shrimp, shelled and
deveined

½ pound small fresh
mushrooms or 1 small can
(8 ounces) button
mushrooms, drained

½ cup sliced bamboo shoots

2 green onions (including
tops), cut diagonally into
2-inch pieces

1 tablespoon cornstarch
mixed with 2 tablespoons
water

Vegetable oil for deep-
frying

12 pieces (about 4 ounces
total) rice crusts, cut into
2-inch squares

Preparation

Soak dried mushrooms in enough warm water to cover for 30 minutes; drain. Cut off and discard stems; thinly slice caps. Set aside.

Combine sauce ingredients in a bowl and set aside.

Cooking

Place a wok or wide frying pan over high heat until hot. Add 2 tablespoons oil, swirling to coat sides. Add pork; stir-fry for about 2 minutes or until lightly browned. Add shrimp; cook and toss for 1 minute more or until shrimp turn pink. Remove pork and shrimp from wok and set aside. Add black mushrooms, fresh mushrooms, bamboo shoots, green onions, and sauce to wok. Cook, stirring constantly, for 2 minutes. Add cornstarch solution and cook, stirring, until sauce boils and thickens slightly. Keep warm.

Set clean wok in a ring stand and add oil to a depth of 2 inches. Place over high heat until oil reaches about 375°F. Add rice crusts, half at a time, and deep-fry for 15 to 20 seconds or until puffy, turning constantly. Lift out and drain on paper towels. Cook remaining rice crusts.

Arrange hot rice crusts in a serving bowl; immediately pour stir-fried meat and vegetables over rice crusts so crusts sizzle.

Tips

Rice crusts should be deep-fried at a very high temperature (about 375°F) and should be cooked at the last minute. Be ready to pour over the stir-fry the very instant the crusts are done.

To make your own rice crusts, cook medium or short-grain rice, using 1 cup rice to 1 cup water. Spread cooked rice into a ¼-inch-thick layer in a greased shallow baking pan; cut into 2-inch squares with a wet knife. Bake in a 350°F oven for 45 minutes to 1 hour or until rice squares are firm and dry.

Pictured on page 66

FISH WITH SPICY TOMATO SAUCE

Makes: 4 servings
Cooking time: 12 minutes

Marinade

1 tablespoon dry sherry
2 green onions (including tops), cut diagonally into 1-inch pieces
1 teaspoon minced fresh ginger
1 egg white, lightly beaten
½ teaspoon salt

1 pound white fish fillets (such as cod, red snapper, or sole), cut into 1½- by 2-inch pieces

Tomato Sauce

½ cup chicken broth
¼ cup *each* tomato paste and crushed pineapple, drained
2 tablespoons packed brown sugar
1 tablespoon rice vinegar or white wine vinegar
2 teaspoons soy sauce
1 teaspoon sesame oil
¼ teaspoon chili oil
3 or 4 dried whole red chili peppers
1½ teaspoons cornstarch mixed with 1 tablespoon water

Cornstarch for coating

Vegetable oil for deep-frying

Tomato wedges and pineapple slices for garnish (optional)

Preparation

Combine marinade ingredients in a bowl. Add fish; stir to coat. Set aside for 30 minutes.

Combine tomato sauce ingredients in a small saucepan. Set aside.

Cooking

Drain fish briefly, pushing green onion pieces aside. Coat with cornstarch, shaking off excess. Set wok in a ring stand and add oil to a depth of 1½ to 2 inches. Place over high heat until oil reaches about 375°F. Add fish, 4 or 5 pieces at a time, and deep-fry for 2 to 3 minutes or until fish is golden brown on outside and opaque in center, turning occasionally. Lift out and drain on paper towels. Arrange fish on a heatproof serving platter and keep warm in a 200°F oven while cooking remaining fish pieces.

Meanwhile, bring tomato sauce to a boil over medium-high heat, stirring constantly. Reduce heat to low; cook, stirring until sauce boils and thickens slightly.

Pour tomato sauce over fish. Garnish with tomato wedges and pineapple slices, if desired.

Tips

Fish can be either deep-fried or pan-fried.

Pictured on page 86

Martin Yan, The Chinese Chef

KUNG PAO SHRIMP

Makes: 4 servings
Cooking time: 5 minutes

Marinade

2 tablespoons *each* soy
sauce and chicken broth

2 teaspoons sesame oil

1 teaspoon cornstarch
mixed with 2 teaspoons
water

¾ pound raw medium-size
shrimp, shelled and
deveined

Kung Pao Sauce

⅓ cup chicken broth

2 tablespoons rice vinegar
or red wine vinegar

1 tablespoon dark soy sauce

1 tablespoon soy sauce

2 teaspoons *each* sweet
bean paste and sugar

1½ teaspoons sesame oil

1 teaspoon cornstarch

2 tablespoons vegetable oil

½ small onion, sliced

1 dried whole red chili
pepper, minced

1 can (8 ounces) sliced
bamboo shoots, drained

1 green bell pepper, seeded
and cut into 1-inch
squares

Preparation

Combine marinade ingredients in a medium-size
bowl. Add shrimp; stir to coat. Cover and refrigerate
for 1 to 2 hours, stirring occasionally.

Combine sauce ingredients in a small bowl and set
aside.

Cooking

Place a wok or wide frying pan over high heat until
hot. Add oil, swirling to coat sides. Add onion; cook,
stirring, until limp and translucent. Add shrimp; stir-
fry for 1 minute or until shrimp turns pink. Add chili
pepper, bamboo shoots, and bell pepper; cook and
toss for 1 minute. Add kung pao sauce; cook,
stirring, until sauce boils and thickens slightly.
Transfer to a serving platter and serve hot.

Pictured on page 86

Szechuan/Hunan

The Chinese name for chopsticks is *fai jee* which translates as "quick little boys." These versatile utensils symbolize speed and agility and have multiple uses in the Chinese kitchen and at the table.

With a little practice, you'll discover that chopsticks are not difficult to use. Start by placing the first chopstick through the crook formed by the thumb and index finger; let the stick rest on the tip of the fourth finger (ring finger) holding the chopstick stationary. Hold the second stick as if you were holding a pencil. Now, move the second chopstick up and down in a pivoting motion bringing its tip in contact with the tip of the stationary chopstick.

The simple design of the chopstick allows you to cook, serve, and eat your Chinese meals in true Chinese style.

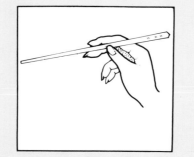

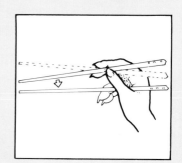

Place first chopstick through crock between thumb and index finger. Hold second chopstick like a pencil. Move second chopstick up and down, bringing tips of chopsticks together to pick up pieces of food.

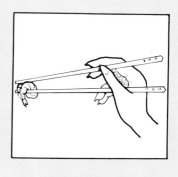

STEAMED WHOLE SPICY CHICKEN

Makes: 4 to 6 servings
Cooking time: 40 minutes

- 1 frying chicken (about 3 pounds), cleaned
- 1 teaspoon salt
- 12 toasted Szechuan peppercorns
- 1 shallot, coarsely chopped
- 1 tablespoon 1-inch slivers fresh ginger

Dipping Sauce

- ¼ cup soy sauce
- 3 tablespoons rice vinegar
- 2 tablespoons sesame oil
- 1 clove garlic, minced
- ½ teaspoon *each* minced fresh ginger and sugar
- ¼ teaspoon ground toasted Szechuan peppercorns

Preparation

Lightly rub chicken inside and out with salt. In a small bowl, combine peppercorns, shallot, and ginger. Rub mixture inside chicken body cavity. Cover and refrigerate for 2 to 4 hours.

Combine dipping sauce ingredients in a small bowl and set aside.

Cooking

Place chicken, breast side up, in a heatproof dish. Set dish in a steamer or on a rack in a wok. Cover and steam over boiling water for 30 to 40 minutes or until meat near thighbone is no longer pink when slashed. Carefully lift chicken from steamer and let cool to room temperature.

Remove and discard skin from chicken, if desired. Hand-shred chicken and arrange on a serving platter. Serve hot or cold with dipping sauce.

Tips

This easy-to-prepare dish is wonderful for last-minute picnics.

Martin Yan, The Chinese Chef

CLOCKWISE FROM TOP: *Szechuan Cucumber Salad (page 70); Zha Jiang Mein (page 92); Fruit & Snow Mushrooms (page 96); and Kung Pao Shrimp, Cheng-Du Dumplings with Peanut Sauce (page 73), and Fish with Spicy Tomato Sauce (page 82).*

Szechuan/Hunan

SMOKE TEA DUCK

Makes: 6 servings
Cooking time: 1¾ hours

1 duckling (4 to 5 pounds),
cleaned

Marinade

2 green onions (including
tops), cut into thirds

3 whole star anise, broken

3 tablespoons dry sherry

2 tablespoons salt

1 tablespoon minced fresh
ginger

2 teaspoons ground toasted
Szechuan peppercorns

¼ cup black tea leaves

3 tablespoons uncooked
rice

2½ tablespoons packed
brown sugar

Vegetable oil for deep-
frying

Green onion slivers, for
garnish

Preparation

Cut off and discard excess neck skin from duck. Remove and discard fat from around body cavity; cut off tail. Prick duck all over with a bamboo skewer. Combine marinade ingredients in a large bowl. Add duck; rub duck inside and out with marinade. Cover and refrigerate overnight.

Cooking

Place duck, breast side up, on a heatproof dish. Set dish in a steamer or on a rack in a wok. Cover and steam over boiling water for 1 hour. Remove duck from steamer and pat dry.

Meanwhile, line a large wok and its lid with foil. Combine tea leaves, rice, and sugar in a small bowl; mix well and place on bottom of the foil-lined wok. Set a rack in the wok; place duck, breast side up, on top of the rack. Cover and cook over medium-high heat for 5 to 6 minutes; turn off heat for 6 to 8 minutes. Cook again for 6 more minutes. Let stand, covered, for 10 minutes. Remove duck, drain well, and let cool for 10 minutes.

Set wok in a ring stand and add oil to a depth of 1½ to 2 inches. Place over medium-high heat until oil reaches about 360°F. Carefully lower duck into oil and deep-fry for 10 minutes, using a ladle to pour oil over duck to brown evenly. Carefully, lift out duck with a large wire strainer or 2 spatulas and drain on paper towels.

Cut duck into serving-size pieces. Place duck pieces on a serving platter, arranging them in the shape of a whole duck. Sprinkle with green onion slivers.

Pictured on page 67

Martin Yan, The Chinese Chef

PRESSED BEAN CURD WITH BEEF

Makes: 4 servings
Cooking time: 4 minutes

½ pound flank steak

Marinade

1 tablespoon *each* soy sauce
and dry sherry
2 teaspoons cornstarch
Dash of Chinese five-spice

Sauce

2 tablespoons water
1 tablespoon *each* soy sauce
and dry sherry
1 teaspoon sesame oil

2 tablespoons vegetable oil
2 stalks celery, cut into 2-
inch matchstick pieces
2 green onions (including
tops), cut diagonally into
2-inch pieces
1 package (7 ounces)
pressed soy bean cake, cut
into thin slices

Preparation

Trim and discard excess fat from beef. Cut beef across the grain into 2-inch matchstick pieces. Combine marinade ingredients in a small bowl. Add beef; stir to coat. Set aside for 30 minutes.

Combine sauce ingredients in a bowl and set aside.

Cooking

Place a wok or wide frying pan over high heat until hot. Add oil, swirling to coat sides. Add beef; stir-fry for 1½ minutes. Remove beef to a bowl and set aside. Add celery, green onions, soy bean cake slices, and sauce; cook, stirring, for 1 minute. Return beef to wok; stir and toss for 1 more minute. Transfer beef to a serving platter. Serve hot.

BRAISED OXTAIL WITH NOODLES

Makes: 4 servings
Cooking time: 2¾ to 3 hours

> 6 pieces oxtail (about 1½ pounds total)

Braising Sauce

> 3 cups Basic Chicken Broth (page 106)
> ¼ cup dry sherry or Shao Hsing wine
> 3 tablespoons soy sauce
> 2 tablespoons hoisin sauce
> 1 tablespoon brown bean paste
> 3 cloves garlic, minced
> 2 green onions (white part only), cut diagonally into 2-inch pieces
> ½ teaspoon toasted Szechuan peppercorns

> 16 cups water
> 1 pound fresh noodles
> ½ cup cold water
> 2 teaspoons sesame oil
> 2 teaspoons cornstarch mixed with 1 tablespoon water

Preparation

Place oxtail in a large pot with enough water to cover and bring to a boil. Then reduce heat and simmer for 5 to 6 minutes. Rinse under cold running water, drain well, and set aside. Combine braising sauce ingredients in a 4-quart ovenproof casserole dish. Add oxtails; stir to coat.

Cooking

Bake oxtails in a 350°F oven for 2½ to 3 hours or until oxtails are tender.

Meanwhile, cut noodles into 6-inch lengths. Bring 16 cups water to a boil in a large pot. Add noodles, stirring to separate strands. When water returns to a boil, add ½ cup cold water. Return to a boil again and cook, stirring, for 2 to 3 minutes or until noodles are tender to bite. Pour into a colander, rinse under cold running water and drain well. Toss noodles with sesame oil. Transfer noodles to a serving platter and set aside.

Remove oxtails from casserole and arrange over noodles. Pour remaining braising sauce through a fine strainer into a bowl. Pour 1 cup of the sauce into a saucepan and bring to a boil. Add cornstarch solution and cook, stirring, until sauce boils and thickens slightly. Pour sauce over oxtail noodles and serve hot.

Tips

Use extra sauce as an all-purpose seasoning sauce for stir-fried dishes. This sauce can also be used many times to braise meat and poultry. With each use, the flavor becomes more complex. Refrigerate cooled sauce in a jar for up to 2 weeks, or freeze for longer storage.

Martin Yan, The Chinese Chef

In China, resources are scarce, and the overpopulated country cannot afford to be wasteful with any commodity—especially food. Neither ingredients nor leftover food are thrown away, but are recycled to make "new dishes" for the next meal.

Nutritional and delicious dishes can be prepared with leftovers. Here are some suggestions:

DEEP-FRIED FOODS such as spring rolls or wontons can be reheated in a 350°F oven until warm or re-fried in hot oil.

STIR-FRIED FOODS with similar tastes can be combined and quickly stir-fried in a wok (though the vegetables may lose a bit of their color and texture). A microwave can also be used to reheat stir-fried or braised foods.

STEAMED FOODS such as dim sum or Mandarin pancakes can be reheated in the steamer. Extras can be sealed in a plastic bag and frozen up to one month.

RICE can be reheated in the steamer or microwave. One of the tastiest ways to use it is to make fried rice, or you can simply add it to soup.

TOFU OR BEAN CURD can be added to soup or a stir-fried dish, or deep-fried tofu cubes can be added to a green salad.

SMITHFIELD HAM, BARBECUED PORK, OR CHINESE SAUSAGE can be sliced or cut into matchstick pieces and stir-fried, then added to fried rice, tossed noodles, omelets, or added to your favorite soup.

"In China, where resources are scarce, leftover food is never thrown away."

ZHA JIANG MEIN

Makes: 6 to 8 servings
Cooking time: 10 minutes

Sauce

- ½ cup chicken broth
- ⅓ cup brown bean sauce
- 1 tablespoon dry sherry
- 2 teaspoons Szechuan chili paste (optional)

- 2 tablespoons dried shrimp
- 1 pound fresh noodles
- 16 cups water
- ½ cup cold water
- 2 tablespoons *each* sesame oil and vegetable oil
- 3 cloves garlic, minced
- ¾ pound ground lean pork
- 1 tablespoon cornstarch mixed with 2 tablespoons water

Garnish

- 2 green onions (including tops), cut into 2-inch slivers
- ½ cucumber, peeled, seeded, and cut into matchstick pieces
- 2 small carrots, blanched and cut into matchstick pieces
- 2 ounces Szechuan preserved vegetables, cut into slivers (optional)
- ½ cup coarsely chopped unsalted roasted peanuts

Preparation

Combine sauce ingredients in a small bowl and set aside.

Soak shrimp in enough warm water to cover for 30 minutes; drain well. Coarsely chop shrimp and set aside.

Cut noodles into 6-inch lengths. Bring 16 cups water to a boil in a large pot. Add noodles, stirring to separate strands. When water returns to a boil, add ½ cup cold water. Return to a boil again and cook, stirring, for 2 to 3 minutes or until noodles are tender to bite. Pour into a colander, rinse under cold running water, and drain well. Toss noodles with 1 tablespoon of the sesame oil. Set aside.

Cooking

Place a wok or wide frying pan over high heat until hot. Add oil, swirling to coat sides. Add garlic and cook, stirring, until fragrant. Add pork and shrimp; stir-fry for 3 to 4 minutes or until pork is browned. Add sauce; cook and toss for 1 minute. Add cornstarch solution and cook, stirring, until sauce boils and thickens slightly.

To serve, place noodles in individual serving bowls. Arrange green onions, cucumber, carrots, and pickles on top of noodles. Spoon meat sauce over noodles and sprinkle with peanuts.

Tips

Wheat-flour noodles are a staple in Northern China.

This can be a wonderful snack served cold, or as a warm hearty one-dish meal.

Pictured on page 87

SPICY CHILLED NOODLES

Makes: 4 to 6 servings
Cooking time: 5 minutes

Sauce:

2 teaspoons sesame seeds
2 tablespoons *each* rice vinegar and soy sauce
2 tablespoons shredded Szechuan preserved vegetables
1 tablespoon sesame oil
2 teaspoons Szechuan chili paste
½ teaspoon garlic salt

1 pound fresh noodles
16 cups water
½ cup cold water
2 tablespoons sesame oil

Preparation

In a wide frying pan, toast sesame seeds over medium heat for about 5 minutes or until golden brown, shaking pan frequently. Combine sesame seeds with remaining sauce ingredients in a bowl; mix well and set aside.

Cooking

Cut noodles into 6-inch lengths. Bring 16 cups water to a boil in a large pot. Add noodles, stirring to separate strands. When water returns to a boil, add ½ cup cold water. Return to a boil again, and cook, stirring, for 2 to 3 minutes or until noodles are tender to bite. Pour into a colander, rinse under cold running water, and drain well. Transfer noodles to a serving bowl. Add sauce and toss well. Cover and refrigerate. Serve cold.

Tips
These noodles are perfect as a side dish. To serve as a main dish, add stir-fried meat and vegetables of your choice.

Whatever your choice of *chiew*, may I offer this toast to you: "Kan Pei!"

The Western palate, although familiar with the cuisine of China, is not so well acquainted with that country's wines.

Chinese wine (or *chiew*, a term that includes all Chinese alcoholic beverages) ranges from Mao Tai, a strong, distilled, vodka-like liquor (up to 120–150 proof) to the more palatable Shao Hsing wine, made in the eastern province of Zhejiang (Chekiang). The latter, made from fermented rice and served warm, is somewhat similar in taste to Japanese sake.

Szechuan/Hunan

Chiew has a history reaching back some 4,000 years. Though wine was lauded by ancient Chinese poets and scholars, many men have met their fate by way of wine. One of the more famous examples is the "Drunken Dragon," the Tang dynasty poet Li Po, who himself drowned while attempting to rescue the moon from drowning. Nevertheless, wine has always been as important in the preparation of Chinese dishes for its aroma, flavor, and hastening of cooking time, as it has been at the table.

Since many traditional Chinese wines are not readily available in North America, we can comfortably substitute dry sherry for Shao Hsing wine when preparing most dishes, and a myriad of fine American, French, German, and Italian wines for drinking.

The many flavors and textures present in China's diverse cuisine allow a lot of freedom when selecting wines. But, here is a rule of thumb to consider: The lighter, more delicate cuisines, such as those of Guangzhou (Canton) and Fujian (Fukien), require fruity white wines including Riesling, Colombard, and Chenin Blanc; the spicier, more substantial dishes from the western provinces, Sichuan and Hunan, ask for medium red wines, such as Burgundy or Chianti; and the northern province flavors (Peking-style) fall somewhere in between and are best accompanied by lighter reds such as Beaujolais. The Chinese-style Western recipes in the Nouvelle Chinese section allow one to choose according to taste.

When planning your menu, don't forget that favorite of both West and East, a cold, light, golden beer.

Whatever your choice, may we offer this toast to start your meal: "Kan Pei!" (Bottoms up!)

COCONUT RICE DUMPLING SOUP

Makes: 4 to 6 servings
Cooking time: 6 minutes

Filling

2 tablespoons sesame seeds

½ cup sweetened shredded coconut

1 tablespoon *each* sugar and minced candied ginger

Dough

1½ cups glutinous rice flour

⅓ cup boiling water

2 tablespoons cold water

16 cups water

½ cup cold water

Sweet Soup

2 cups water

½ cup sugar

Preparation

In a wide frying pan, toast sesame seeds over medium heat for about 5 minutes or until golden brown, shaking pan frequently. Grind sesame seeds with a mortar and pestle, or place in a blender and whirl until ground. Place ground sesame seeds in a bowl and add remaining filling ingredients; mix well. Set aside.

Measure rice flour into a bowl. Make a well in the center of flour and pour boiling water into well, stirring with chopsticks or a fork until dough is evenly moistened. Add cold water and stir until dough forms a ball.

On a lightly floured surface, knead dough for about 5 minutes or until smooth and shiny. Cover with a damp cloth and let rest for 10 minutes. Roll dough into a 12-inch-long cylinder. Cut cylinder crosswise into 1-inch pieces. Dust palms of hands lightly with rice flour and roll each piece into a ball.

To shape each dumpling, flatten one ball of dough with a rolling pin to make a 2½-inch circle, keeping remaining dough covered to prevent drying. Place ½ teaspoon of filling in center of each circle. Gather and pinch edges together at the top to seal securely. Roll carefully between your palms to form a round ball. Cover filled dumplings with a damp cloth while filling remaining dumplings. (There will be some filling left over)

Cooking

In a large pot, bring 16 cups water to a boil. Add dumplings, without crowding, stirring to separate. When water returns to a boil, add ½ cup cold water. Return to a boil again and cook, stirring for 5 minutes until dumplings start to float. Lift out dumplings with a wire strainer and place in a colander to drain. Cook remaining dumplings.

Meanwhile, prepare sweet soup. In a small saucepan, combine water and sugar. Place over medium heat, swirling pan occasionally, until sugar is dissolved. When soup begins to boil, remove from heat.

Place dumplings in individual bowls. Pour soup over dumplings and serve hot.

Tips

Dumplings can also be steamed over boiling water for 8 minutes.

For a variation, lightly coat cooked dumplings in remaining filling. Serve hot as a snack or a dessert.

FRUIT & SNOW MUSHROOMS

Makes: 4 servings
Cooking time: 40 minutes

1 ounce dried snow mushrooms (white fungus)
1 can (10 ounces) mandarin orange segments
1 can (11 ounces) lychee fruit
1 can (8 ounces) chunk pineapple
4 cups water

Syrup

¾ cup *each* water and sugar
1 teaspoon Triple Sec

Sweetened whipped cream (optional)

Preparation

Soak snow mushrooms in enough warm water to cover for 1 hour. Cut off and discard hard stems. Set mushrooms aside.

Drain all fruits, then place in a large serving bowl; set aside.

Cooking

Place snow mushrooms in a medium-size saucepan and pour in enough water to cover; bring to a boil. Reduce heat, cover, and simmer for 30 minutes; drain.

Meanwhile, combine ¾ cup water and sugar in a small saucepan; place over medium heat, swirling pan occasionally, until sugar is dissolved. Continue to cook until syrup is reduced by one-half, stirring constantly. Remove from heat, then stir in Triple Sec. Let cool.

Add snow mushrooms to fruit. Pour in cooled syrup; toss well. Cover and refrigerate until chilled. Serve in individual bowls; top with whipped cream, if desired.

Tips

Snow mushrooms (white fungus), packaged in clear plastic boxes, are frilly, golden, and transparent. They are usually used in soups and in desserts.

Pictured on page 87

PEANUT-FILLED SNOW PUFFS

Makes: 20 snow puffs
Cooking time: 10 minutes

- 2 tablespoons sesame seeds
- 3 tablespoons butter
- ⅓ cup sugar
- ½ cup finely chopped unsalted roasted peanuts
  All-purpose flour for coating

Egg White Mixture

- 6 egg whites
- ¼ teaspoon cornstarch

  Vegetable oil for deep-frying

Preparation

In a wide frying pan, toast sesame seeds over medium heat for about 5 minutes or until golden brown, shaking pan frequently. Grind sesame seeds with a mortar and pestle, or place in a blender and whirl until ground. Set aside.

Melt butter in a medium-size saucepan over low heat. Add sugar and cook, stirring constantly, for about 1 minute or until sugar is dissolved. Remove saucepan from heat. Add ground sesame seeds and peanuts; mix well. Divide mixture into 20 equal pieces. Roll each piece carefully between your palms to form a round ball. Evenly coat each ball with flour, shaking off excess. Set aside.

To prepare egg white mixture, beat egg whites until moist, stiff peaks form when beaters are lifted. Fold in cornstarch.

Drop flour-coated balls, one at a time, into egg white mixture. Using two soup spoons, turn balls so they are thickly coated with egg white and resemble a snow puff.

Cooking

Set wok in a ring stand and add oil to a depth of 1½ to 2 inches. Place over medium-high heat until oil reaches about 350°F. Add puffs, 4 or 5 at a time, and deep-fry for 2 minutes or until golden brown, turning occasionally. Lift out and drain on paper towels. Keep cooked puffs warm in a 200°F oven while cooking remaining puffs. Serve hot.

Tips

This unique dessert is normally served at banquets.

Substitute chopped almonds or chopped pecans for the peanuts.

PEKING

Peking has always been a bustling center for trade and government. Sophisticated menus, influenced by the Imperial Court and its lavish banquet-style dining, produced an unusually refined style of regional cooking.

CLOKWISE FROM RIGHT: Sweet Bean Paste Puffs (page 127), Twice-fried Shredded Beef (page 121), and Peking Pork & Mushroom Soup (page 108); Mandarin Glazed Apples (page 126); Chicken Foo Yung (page 110); and Fish Rolls in Wine Sauce (page 114).

**"Food from Peking
is highly refined.
You can trace
the origin
of many recipes to
the Imperial Court."**

Referred to as the cradle of civilization because of Peking Man (400,000 B.C.), this area also remained the home of the Imperial Court for several hundred years. The area's cuisine includes highly refined recipes from all of China's regions.

Beijing (Peking) has been the center of trade and government for much of China's history, and cultural life thrives in this bustling metropolis. The old Imperial Court was the major supporter of cultural life in days gone by, and this patronage included many lavish banquets, utilizing the skills of hundreds of chefs and assistants from throughout the land. The culinary arts thrived there. Shandong (Shantung) province, the birthplace of Confucius, also brought forth master chef Yi Ya.

Commonly called Peking-style, the cooking of the region is characterized by tangy sweet and sour sauces and the famous technique of preparing Peking duck. Interestingly, Peking-style includes many Mongolian dishes due to its northwest bordering neighbor, Inner Mongolia. Best known are the Mongolian Hot Pot, a cooking method similar to fondue, and lamb dishes which have become popular throughout China.

The winds that sweep down from the northernmost regions make the growing season short and far too cold and dry to grow rice. Oats, wheat, and soybeans are primary crops in the region, and the noodles, dumplings, rolls, and breads that accompany meals are usually made from one of these three.

Seasoning, of course, is an important part of the northern cuisine. Particularly useful are garlic, ginger, and green onions. The most popular cooking techniques are steaming, baking, and *bao* or "explode-frying," in which foods are cooked in smoking-hot oil.

The different varieties of ingredients and cooking techniques found in northern China's cuisine make for a delightful change of pace.

SUGGESTED MENUS

Peking Pork & Mushroom Soup
Jellied Spiced Beef
Sweet & Sour Pork
Mandarin Glazed Apples

Peking-Style Eggplant
Chicken Foo Yung
Twice-Fried Shredded Beef
Sweet Bean Paste Puff

Hot & Sour Soup
Pot Stickers
Steamed Ginger Chicken
Fish Rolls in Wine Sauce

POT STICKERS

Makes: 28 pot stickers
Cooking time: 20 minutes

Filling

    5 dried black mushrooms
    ½ pound ground lean pork
    2 green onions (including tops), finely chopped
    1¼ cups finely shredded Chinese (napa) cabbage
    1 tablespoon *each* soy sauce, dry sherry, and cornstarch
    2 teaspoons sesame oil
    1 teaspoon minced fresh ginger
    ½ teaspoon sugar

Dough

    3 cups all-purpose flour
    1⅓ cups boiling water

    2 tablespoons vegetable oil
    ⅔ cup chicken broth

    Soy sauce

    Rice vinegar

    Chili oil

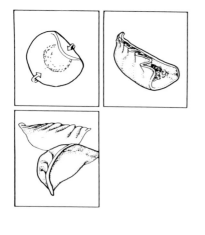

Preparation

Soak mushrooms in enough warm water to cover for 30 minutes; drain. Cut off and discard stems; finely chop caps. Combine mushrooms with remaining filling ingredients in a medium-size bowl; mix well.

Measure flour into a large bowl. Mix in boiling water, stirring with chopsticks or a fork until dough is evenly moistened. Cover and let rest for 30 minutes.

On a lightly floured surface, knead dough for about 5 minutes or until smooth and elastic. Divide dough in half. Roll each half into a 14-inch-long cylinder. Cut each cylinder crosswise into 1-inch pieces; shape each piece into a ball.

To shape each pot sticker, flatten one ball of dough with a rolling pin to make a 3-inch circle, keeping remaining dough covered to prevent drying. Place 1 heaping teaspoon of filling in center of each circle (see illustration). Lightly moisten edges of circle with water. Fold circle in half over filling to form a semicircle. Starting at one end, pinch curved edges together; make 4 to 6 pleats along the edge facing you, pressing edges to seal securely. Set pot sticker down firmly, seam side up. Cover filled pot stickers with a damp cloth while shaping remaining pot stickers.

Cooking

Place a wide frying pan with a nonstick finish over medium-high heat until hot. Add 1 tablespoon of the oil, swirling to coat sides. Set half the pot stickers, seam side up, without crowding, in frying pan. Cook for 2 to 2½ minutes or until bottoms are golden brown, swirling pan occasionally to ensure even browning. Drain excess oil and reduce heat to medium-low. Pour in ⅓ cup of the broth; cover and cook for 5 to 6 minutes or until liquid has evaporated, swirling pan occasionally. Transfer pot stickers to a serving platter and keep warm in a 200°F oven. Cook remaining pot stickers with remaining oil and broth.

Martin Yan, The Chinese Chef

Mix soy sauce, rice vinegar and chili oil in a combination to suit your taste, then serve as a dipping sauce to accompany pot stickers.

Pictured on page 118

CRISPY SHRIMP WITH SAUCES

Makes: 4 servings
Cooking time: 20 minutes

 ¾ pound medium-size raw shrimp

Marinade

 1 teaspoon dry sherry
 ½ teaspoon salt
 Dash of white pepper

Batter

 ¾ cup all-purpose flour
 ¼ cup cornstarch
 1¼ teaspoons baking powder
 ½ teaspoon sugar (optional)
 ¾ cup cold water or flat beer
 1 teaspoon vegetable oil

Ketchup Dip

 ¼ cup ketchup
 1 teaspoon Worcestershire sauce
 ½ teaspoon chili oil

Soy-Mustard Dip

 ¼ cup soy sauce
 2 teaspoons Hot Mustard Sauce (page 32)

 Vegetable oil for deep-frying

 Parsley sprigs, for garnish
 Lemon wedges, for garnish

Preparation

Shell shrimp, leaving tails attached. Split each shrimp along back, cutting almost through to make shrimp lie flat; devein. Rinse and pat dry with paper towels.

In a medium-size bowl, combine marinade ingredients. Add shrimp; stir to coat. Set aside for 30 minutes.

Measure flour, cornstarch, sugar, and baking powder into a medium-size bowl; mix well. Gradually add cold water and oil, beating with a wire whisk until smooth.

Combine ingredients for ketchup dip and soy-mustard dip in separate bowls, blending well. Set aside.

Cooking

Set wok in a ring stand and add oil to a depth of 2 inches. Place over high heat until oil reaches about 375°F. Dip shrimp, a few at a time, into batter, allowing excess batter to drip off. Add shrimp, without crowding, and deep-fry for 3 to 4 minutes or until golden brown, turning occasionally. Lift out and drain on paper towels. Arrange cooked shrimp in a heatproof serving platter and keep warm in a 200°F oven while cooking remaining shrimp.

Garnish with parsley and lemon wedges. Serve with ketchup dip and soy-mustard dip.

Tips

To deep-fry shrimp in advance, cook only until lightly browned. Re-fry shrimp over high heat (360° to 375°F) for 1 ½ to 2 minutes just before serving. The second frying may make the shrimp crispier.

Pictured on page 119

Peking

SPICY GREEN BEAN SALAD

Makes: 4 servings
Cooking time: 10 minutes

Dressing

- 1 green onion (white part only), minced
- 2½ tablespoons soy sauce
- 2 tablespoons rice vinegar
- 4 teaspoons sesame oil
- 1 tablespoon vegetable oil
- 2 teaspoons minced garlic
- 1 teaspoon sugar
- ¾ teaspoon cornstarch mixed with 1½ teaspoons water
- ½ teaspoon *each* dried red chili flakes and chili oil

- 1 pound green beans
- 4 cups water
- ¼ teaspoon salt
- 1 teaspoon vegetable oil

Preparation

Combine dressing ingredients in a small saucepan. Set aside.

Remove ends and strings of green beans, then cut diagonally into 2-inch pieces.

Cooking

Bring water, salt, and oil to a boil in medium-size saucepan. Blanch beans in boiling water for 6 to 8 minutes or until tender to bite. Rinse under cold running water; drain well.

Bring dressing to a boil over medium-high heat. Cook, stirring, until dressing thickens slightly. Add beans to dressing, tossing to coat well.

Cover and refrigerate. Serve cold.

Tips

For an easy variation, substitute asparagus or Chinese yard-long beans for the green beans.

Pictured on page 119

HOT & SOUR SOUP

Makes: 6 to 8 servings
Cooking time: 10 minutes

4 dried black mushrooms
1 tablespoon dried shrimp
8 to 10 cloud ears
6 to 8 tiger lily buds
6 cups Basic Chicken Broth (page 106)
¼ pound boneless lean pork, cut into matchstick pieces
½ cup matchstick pieces bamboo shoots
6 tablespoons rice vinegar
¼ cup soy sauce
1 teaspoon sesame oil
¾ teaspoon *each* white pepper and chili oil
½ teaspoon sugar
3 tablespoons cornstarch mixed with ¼ cup water
1 egg, lightly beaten
Salt

1 green onion (including top), cut into 1-inch slivers, for garnish
1 tablespoon chopped cilantro (Chinese parsley) leaves, for garnish

Preparation

Soak mushrooms in enough warm water to cover for 30 minutes; drain, reserving juice. Soak shrimp, cloud ears, and tiger lily buds separately in enough warm water to cover for 30 minutes; drain well. Cut off and discard mushroom stems; thinly slice caps. Cut off hard knobby ends of lily buds and tie each bud into a knot. Set mushrooms, shrimp, cloud ears, and lily buds aside.

Cooking

In a large pot, bring broth and reserved mushroom juice to a boil over medium-high heat. Add pork, mushrooms, shrimp, cloud ears, lily buds, and bamboo shoots. Cook, stirring occasionally, for 3 minutes.

Stir in vinegar, soy sauce, sesame oil, white pepper, chili oil, and sugar; return to a boil. Reduce heat, and simmer, stirring constantly, for 3 more minutes. Add cornstarch solution and cook, stirring, until soup boils and thickens slightly. Remove soup from heat and slowly drizzle in egg, stirring constantly. Season to taste with salt. Serve soup hot, in individual bowls. Garnish with green onion and cilantro.

Tips

To achieve a nice smooth egg flower consistency, do not overbeat egg.

Adjust hotness of the soup by adjusting the white pepper and chili oil to your liking.

Substitute shredded chicken, ham, or canned abalone for the pork, if desired.

Try adding vinegar at the last minute to retain the maximum aroma.

BASIC CHICKEN BROTH

Makes: About 10 cups
Cooking time: 2 hours

 2 pounds raw chicken
 bones (necks, backs, or
 any other uncooked
 bones)
 4 thin slices fresh ginger,
 each 1 by 2 inches
 2 green onions (including
 tops), cut in half
 3 quarts water
 Salt

Cooking

Combine chicken bones, ginger, green onions and water in a large pot. Bring to a boil then reduce heat and simmer, uncovered, for 2 hours. Skim and discard fat from broth. Pour broth through a large strainer into a bowl; discard residue. Salt to taste when ready to use.

RICH CLASSIC CHICKEN BROTH

Makes: About 10 cups
Cooking time: 3 hours

 2 pounds raw chicken
 bones (necks, backs or
 any other uncooked
 bones)
 1½ to 2 pounds pork
 spareribs or bones
 1 pound ham bone
 (optional)
 4 thin slices fresh ginger,
 each 1- by 2-inches
 2 green onions (including
 tops)
 3 quarts water
 Salt

Cooking

Combine chicken bones, pork bones, ham bone, ginger, green onions, and water in a large pot. Bring to a boil, then reduce heat and simmer, uncovered, for 3 hours. Skim and discard fat from broth. Pour broth through a large strainer into bowl; discard residue. Salt to taste when ready to use.

Martin Yan, The Chinese Chef

PEPPERY FISH SOUP

Makes: 4 to 6 servings
Cooking time: 8 minutes

½ pound white fish fillets (such as cod, sole or sea bass), cut into 1- by 2-inch pieces

½ teaspoon salt

1 egg, lightly beaten

Cornstarch for coating

Vegetable oil for deep-frying

4 cups Basic Chicken Broth (page 106)

1 teaspoon minced fresh ginger

2 cloves garlic, minced

3 tablespoons white wine vinegar

4 teaspoons soy sauce

½ teaspoon sesame oil

⅛ teaspoon white pepper

2 teaspoons chopped

Cilantro (Chinese parsley) leaves, for garnish

Preparation

Sprinkle fish with salt; set aside for 20 minutes. Dip fish pieces into egg. Coat with cornstarch, shaking off excess. Set aside.

Cooking

Set wok in a ring stand and add oil to a depth of 2 inches. Place over medium-high heat until oil reaches about 360°F. Add fish pieces, a few at a time, and deep-fry for 1½ to 2 minutes or until golden brown. Lift out and drain on paper towels. Set aside.

In a large pot, bring broth, ginger, and garlic to a boil over high heat, stirring occasionally. Add fried fish, vinegar, soy sauce, sesame oil, and white pepper; mix well. Reduce heat and simmer for 3 minutes. Pour soup into a tureen and garnish with cilantro.

Tips

The fish can be pan-fried instead of deep-fried before adding to the soup.

Pictured on page 118

PEKING PORK & MUSHROOM SOUP

Makes: 6 to 8 servings
Cooking time: 25 minutes

Marinade

2 teaspoons soy sauce
1 teaspoon dry sherry
½ teaspoon sesame oil

¼ pound boneless lean pork,
   cut into 1- by 2-inch thin
   slices
2 tablespoons dried shrimp
4 dried black mushrooms
¼ cup gingko nuts (optional)
1 tablespoon vegetable oil
1 green onion (including
   top), finely chopped
6 cups Basic Chicken Broth
   (page 106)
¼ cup matchstick pieces
   bamboo shoots
2 ounces Smithfield or
   Virginia ham, cut into 2-
   inch matchstick pieces
½ package (8 ounces) firm
   tofu (bean curd), drained
   and cut into ½-inch cubes
2 tablespoons soy sauce
1 teaspoon sesame oil
   Dash of white pepper
   Salt

Preparation

Combine marinade ingredients in a small bowl. Add pork; stir to coat. Set aside for 30 minutes.

Soak shrimp and mushrooms *separately* in enough warm water to cover for 30 minutes; drain. Cut off and discard stems; thinly slice cap. Set mushrooms and shrimp aside.

If using gingko nuts, place in a small saucepan and add enough water to cover nuts. Bring water to a boil; reduce heat, cover, and simmer for 12 to 15 minutes or until tender to bite. Drain well. Peel off and discard outer skins; set nuts aside.

Cooking

Place a wok or wide frying pan over high heat until hot. Add oil, swirling to coat sides. Add pork, shrimp, and green onion; stir-fry for about 2 minutes or until pork is lightly browned. Set aside.

In a large pot, bring broth to a boil over medium-high heat. Add mushrooms, gingko nuts, bamboo shoots, ham, and tofu. Return to a boil, then reduce heat to medium-low. Add pork mixture, soy sauce, sesame oil, white pepper, and salt to taste. Cook, stirring, for 1 minute. Serve immediately.

Pictured on page 99

108

Martin Yan, The Chinese Chef

NAPA CABBAGE WITH CHINESE SAUSAGE

Makes: 4 to 6 servings
Cooking time: 20 minutes

- 6 dried black mushrooms
- 2 green onions (including tops)
- 2 tablespoons vegetable oil
- 3 cloves garlic, minced
- 1 Chinese sausage (2 ounces), cut diagonally into ¼-inch slices
- 1 Chinese (napa) cabbage (about 1½ pounds), cut into bite-size pieces

Sauce

- ⅓ cup chicken broth
- 3 tablespoons soy sauce
- 1 tablespoon dry sherry
- 2 teaspoons chili paste (optional)
- 1 teaspoon sugar
- ¼ teaspoon salt
- 4 teaspoons cornstarch mixed with 2 tablespoons water

Preparation

Soak mushrooms in enough warm water to cover for 30 minutes; drain. Cut off and discard stems; slice caps in half. Set aside.

Cut white parts and green tops of green onions diagonally into 2-inch pieces; set aside separately.

Combine all sauce ingredients except cornstarch solution in a bowl and set aside.

Cooking

Place a wok or wide frying pan over medium-high heat until hot. Add oil, swirling to coat sides. Add garlic; cook, stirring until fragrant. Add green onions (white parts only) and Chinese sausage; stir-fry for 2 minutes. Add cabbage and sauce; reduce heat, cover, and simmer, stirring occasionally, for 15 minutes or until cabbage is tender to bite. Add cornstarch solution and cook, stirring, until sauce boils and thickens slightly. Toss in green onion tops; mix well. Transfer cabbage to a serving platter and serve hot.

Tips

If you wish, you can substitute Chinese preserved pork for the sausage. Chinese sausages and Chinese preserved pork are available only in Oriental markets.

CHICKEN FOO YUNG

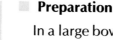

Makes: 4 servings
Cooking time: 10 minutes

Foo Yung

- ½ chicken breast, skinned, boned, and minced
- 1 tablespoon chopped Chinese sausage, Smithfield ham, or Virginia ham
- 3 tablespoons chicken broth
- 2 teaspoons chopped cilantro (Chinese parsley) leaves
- 1 teaspoon minced fresh ginger
- 1 clove garlic, minced
- 2 teaspoons cornstarch
- ½ teaspoon salt
  Dash of white pepper
- 4 egg whites

Sauce

- ½ cup chicken broth
- 1 tablespoon dry sherry
- 1 teaspoon sesame oil
- ⅛ teaspoon salt
- 2 teaspoons cornstarch mixed with 1 tablespoon water

- 4 teaspoons vegetable oil
- 2 green onions (including tops), finely chopped, for garnish

Preparation

In a large bowl, combine all foo yung ingredients except egg whites; mix well. In another bowl, beat egg whites until moist, stiff peaks form when beaters are lifted. Fold half the beaten egg whites into foo yung mixture to lighten it; then gently fold in remaining egg whites. Set aside.

Combine sauce ingredients in a small saucepan and set aside.

Cooking

Place a 10-inch frying pan with a nonstick finish over medium-high heat until hot. Add 1 teaspoon of the oil, swirling to coat sides. Pour one-fourth of the foo yung mixture into pan, tilting pan to coat bottom evenly. Cook for 1½ to 2 minutes or until foo yung sets and becomes fluffy. Arrange foo yung omelets on a heatproof serving dish and keep warm in a 200°F oven while cooking remaining foo yung omelets.

Meanwhile, cook sauce over medium heat, stirring, until sauce boils and thickens slightly.

Pour sauce over omelets and sprinkle green onions on top. Serve hot.

Tips

It is very important to beat egg whites until stiff but not dry. Gradually fold in egg whites with a wire whisk.

Pictured on page 98

STEAMED GINGER CHICKEN

Makes: 4 to 6 servings
Cooking time: 35 minutes

- 1 frying chicken (about 3 pounds)
- 4 teaspoons salt
- 2 tablespoons dry sherry
- 2 tablespoons 1-inch slivers fresh ginger
- 3 green onions (including tops), cut into 1-inch slivers

Sauce

- 3 tablespoons vegetable oil
- 4 teaspoons minced fresh ginger
- 2 green onions (including tops), finely chopped
- 1 tablespoon soy sauce
- 2 teaspoons sesame oil

Preparation

Rub chicken inside and out with salt and sherry. Cover and refrigerate for 1 hour. Then place, breast side up, in a heatproof dish and sprinkle with slivered ginger and green onions.

Cooking

Set dish in a steamer or on a rack in a wok. Cover and steam over boiling water for 30 to 35 minutes or until meat near thighbone is no longer pink when slashed.

Meanwhile, place oil in a saucepan over medium-high heat until hot. Add ginger and green onions; cook, stirring for 30 seconds. Stir in soy sauce and sesame oil until well blended. Keep warm.

Remove and drain chicken. Cut into serving-size pieces and arrange on a large serving platter. Pour sauce over chicken and serve hot.

FIVE-SPICE FRIED CHICKEN

Makes: 4 to 6 servings
Cooking time: 40 minutes

1 frying chicken (about 3
  pounds), cleaned
1½ teaspoons salt

Marinade

3 tablespoons soy sauce
2 tablespoons dry sherry
2 cloves garlic, minced
1 teaspoon *each* minced
  fresh ginger and Chinese
  five-spice
¾ teaspoon sugar

1 egg, lightly beaten
¼ cup all-purpose flour or
  cornstarch

Vegetable oil for deep-
  frying
Five-Spice Salt (page 32)

Preparation

Rub chicken inside and out with salt. Cut into 8 large serving pieces.

Combine marinade ingredients in a large bowl. Add chicken pieces; stir to coat. Cover and refrigerate for at least 4 to 6 hours or overnight.

Cooking

Place chicken in a heatproof dish. Set dish in a steamer or on a rack in a wok. Cover and steam over boiling water for 12 minutes. Remove and let chicken cool.

Dip chicken pieces into egg. Lightly coat with flour, shaking off excess. Set aside.

Set wok in a ring stand and add oil to a depth of 2 inches. Place over medium-high heat until oil reaches about 360°F. Add chicken pieces, a few at a time, and deep-fry for 6 to 8 minutes or until crisp and golden brown, turning frequently. Lift out and drain on paper towels. Keep cooked chicken warm in a 200°F oven while cooking remaining chicken.

Place chicken pieces on a serving platter, arranging them in the shape of a whole chicken. Serve with five-spice salt, if desired.

Tips

After coating chicken in cornstarch-flour mixture, let it set for 3 to 4 minutes to keep coating from separating into flakes while deep-frying. These flakes will burn and make the oil dirty.

Martin Yan, The Chinese Chef

SHANTUNG SHREDDED CHICKEN

Makes: 4 to 6 servings
Cooking time: 40 minutes

3 teaspoons salt

1 teaspoon ground toasted
Szechuan peppercorns
(page 18)

½ teaspoon Chinese five-
spice

1 frying chicken (about 3
pounds), cleaned

Vegetable oil for deep-
frying

2 tablespoons 1-inch slivers
fresh ginger

4 green onions (including
tops), cut into 1-inch
slivers

½ cup chicken broth

2 tablespoons *each* soy
sauce and dry sherry

2 teaspoons sugar

2 teaspoons cornstarch
mixed with 1 tablespoon
water

Cilantro (Chinese
parsley), for garnish

Preparation

Combine 1½ teaspoons of the salt, peppercorns and five-spice in a large bowl. Rub chicken inside and out with mixture. Cover and refrigerate for at least 4 hours or overnight.

Cooking

Set wok in a ring stand and add oil to a depth of 2½ inches. Place over medium-high heat until oil reaches about 360°F. Carefully lower chicken into oil and cook for 4 to 5 minutes or until evenly browned, using a ladle to pour hot oil over chicken. Carefully lift out chicken with a large wire strainer or 2 spatulas; drain on paper towels. Place chicken, breast side up, in a heatproof dish and sprinkle with ginger and green onions.

In a small bowl, combine broth, soy sauce, sherry, sugar, and remaining 1½ teaspoons of the salt; pour over chicken. Set dish in a steamer or on a rack in a wok. Cover and steam over boiling water for about 30 minutes or until meat near thighbone is no longer pink when slashed. Let chicken cool.

Meanwhile, pour juices from steaming dish into a saucepan and bring to a boil over medium-high heat. Add cornstarch solution and cook, stirring, until sauce boils and thickens. Keep warm.

Hand-shred chicken and arrange on a serving platter. Garnish with cilantro and serve with sauce.

Tips

For easier handling when frying, cut chicken in half along the breast and cook 2 half chickens rather than one whole one.

FISH ROLLS IN WINE SAUCE

Makes: 8 rolls
Cooking time: 15 minutes

Filling

6 dried black mushrooms

¼ pound Smithfield or Virginia ham, cut into 2-inch matchstick pieces

½ cup matchstick pieces bamboo shoots

2 green onions (including tops), cut diagonally into 2-inch pieces

1 pound white fish fillets (such as red snapper, cod, carp, or sole)

½ teaspoon salt
Dash of white pepper

2 egg whites, lightly beaten

1 tablespoon cornstarch

½ pound snow peas, ends and strings removed

Sauce

¾ cup chicken broth

⅓ cup dry sherry

2 teaspoons sesame oil

½ teaspoon *each* salt and minced fresh ginger

¼ teaspoon sugar
Dash of white pepper

1 tablespoon cornstarch mixed with 2 tablespoons water

Preparation

Soak mushrooms in enough warm water to cover for 30 minutes; drain. Cut off and discard stems; thinly slice caps. Combine sliced mushroom caps and remaining filling ingredients in a bowl; set aside.

Cut fish into 2- by 5-inch slices. Sprinkle with salt and white pepper. In a small bowl, lightly whisk egg whites and cornstarch. Dip each piece of fish into egg white mixture. Place 1 tablespoon of the filling in center of each piece of fish. Roll up fish, using a toothpick to secure ends. Place in a dish and set aside while filling remaining fish pieces.

In a medium-size saucepan, bring about 1 quart water to boil. Blanch snow peas for 2 to 3 minutes or until crisp-tender. Rinse under cold running water and drain well. Arrange snow peas in a bed on a serving platter; set aside.

Combine all sauce ingredients except cornstarch solution in a saucepan and set aside.

Cooking

Set dish of fish rolls in a steamer or on a rack in a wok. Cover and steam over boiling water for 5 to 6 minutes or until fish turns opaque.

Meanwhile, bring sauce to a boil, stirring constantly. Add cornstarch solution and cook, stirring, until sauce boils and thickens. Keep warm.

Remove toothpicks from fish. Arrange fish rolls on top of snow pea bed. Pour sauce over fish and serve hot.

Pictured on page 98

Martin Yan, The Chinese Chef

SWEET & SOUR PORK

Makes: 4 to 6 servings
Cooking time: 20 minutes

Marinade

1 tablespoon dry sherry

2 teaspoons soy sauce

¼ teaspoon salt

¾ pound boneless lean pork,
  cut into 1-inch cubes

1 egg, lightly beaten

¼ cup *each* all-purpose flour
  and cornstarch
  Vegetable oil for deep-
  frying

Sauce

2 teaspoons vegetable oil

1 clove garlic, minced

½ teaspoon minced fresh
  ginger

¼ cup rice vinegar or cider
  vinegar

¼ cup *each* chicken broth
  and packed brown sugar

3 tablespoons ketchup

2 teaspoons soy sauce

½ teaspoon grated orange or
  lemon peel

1 can (8 ounces) chunk
  pineapple, drained

1 can (11 ounces) lychee
  fruit, drained (optional)

1 small green bell pepper,
  cut into 1-inch squares

1 small red bell pepper, cut
  into 1-inch squares

2½ teaspoons cornstarch
  mixed with 1½
  tablespoons water

Hot cooked rice

Preparation

Combine marinade ingredients in a large bowl. Add pork; stir to coat. Set aside for 30 minutes. Stir egg into marinated pork; mix well and set aside.

In a medium-size bowl, combine flour and cornstarch; mix well. Coat pork cubes with flour-cornstarch mixture, shaking off excess. Let set for 3 to 4 minutes.

Cooking

Set wok in a ring stand and add oil to a depth of 1½ to 2 inches. Place over high heat until oil reaches about 375°F. Add pork cubes, without crowding, and deep-fry for 3 to 4 minutes or until pork is no longer pink when slashed, turning occasionally. Lift out and drain on paper towels. Keep warm in a 200°F oven while cooking remaining pork.

Place clean wok over medium-high heat until hot. Add 2 teaspoons oil, swirling to coat sides. Add garlic and ginger; cook, stirring, until fragrant. Stir in vinegar, broth, brown sugar, ketchup, soy sauce, and orange peel; mix well. Add pineapple, lychee fruit, and bell peppers. Cook and toss for about 1 minute or until vegetables are crisp-tender. Add cornstarch solution and cook, stirring, until sauce boils and thickens.

Add cooked pork cubes to sauce; stir to coat. Place in a serving bowl. Serve over rice.

Tips

To get a head start for entertaining, you may want to deep-fry pork ahead of time and set it aside. Re-fry pork for 1½ to 2 minutes over high heat (360° to 375°F) just before combining it with sauce. (The second frying may give you a crispier texture).

The secret of a good sweet and sour sauce is the proper balance of sugar and vinegar; adjust to your liking.

Eating out in a Chinese restaurant is a great treat. Since Chinese food is meant to be shared, it's more fun to go with several people so you can enjoy a variety of dishes.

For a simple snack, you can walk into a rice or noodle shop and order fried noodles topped with an assortment of meats and condiments, or noodles in broth, or a quick stir-fried dish served over steamed rice.

The most familiar types of Chinese restaurants have a "family-style" menu, offering a wide variety of dishes from simple, traditional entrees to the regional specialties of the chef.

In North American restaurants, there are basically three main regional cuisines: Southern (Cantonese), Northern (Peking or "Mandarin") and Western (Szechuan-Hunan). Although a restaurant may be named after one region, the menu will probably contain well-known dishes from other regions.

When seeking authentic Chinese food, try to choose a place with Chinese patrons. Luckily, there are many such restaurants to choose from.

Chinese restaurants often have daily specials not included on the menu, and sometimes even a separate menu in Chinese that the waiter can interpret for you. Look at what is being served around you; if a dish appeals to you, don't hesitate to ask the waiter what it is.

To choose different types of dishes, keep in mind the flavor, color, texture, and cooking techniques of each choice. One dish should complement the next. Generally, one dish per person plus rice and soup will provide plenty of food. Any leftovers? Don't feel embarrassed to ask for a "doggie bag."

> **"When looking for a restaurant with authentic Chinese food, choose one with Chinese patrons."**

Martin Yan, The Chinese Chef

If you feel truly adventurous, you might want to try a Chinese banquet with a few friends, the best way to explore traditional dishes. Often, in a banquet, 10 to 12 courses are served, one at a time. In China, a person is honored at least three times with banquets: at birth, when he gets married, and after his funeral. Although beyond your first opportunity, and not wishing to hasten the last, you can still arrange a banquet without having to get married!

西樓宴會

Martin Yan, The Chinese Chef

CLOCKWISE FROM TOP RIGHT: Crispy Shrimp with Sauces (page 103); Spicy Green Bean Salad (page 104); chef Martin Yan selecting fish; Pot Stickers (page 102); and Peppery Fish Soup (page 107) with Sesame Biscuits (page 125).

JELLIED SPICED BEEF

Makes: 6 servings
Cooking time: 2 hours

1 pound boneless beef chuck

Braising Sauce

2 cups water
¼ cup *each* dry sherry and soy sauce
2 cloves garlic, minced
3 thin slices fresh ginger, each 1 by 2 inches
3 green onions (including tops), cut diagonally into 2-inch pieces
1 cinnamon stick
2 whole star anise
1½ tablespoons sugar
2 teaspoons sesame oil
1 teaspoon ground toasted Szechuan peppercorns (page 18)
½ teaspoon salt
¼ teaspoon Chinese five-spice

1 tablespoon vegetable oil
2 tablespoons unflavored gelatin (2 envelopes)
½ cup cold water

Cilantro (Chinese parsley) sprigs, for garnish

Preparation

Trim and discard excess fat from beef. Set aside. Combine braising sauce ingredients in a medium-size bowl and set aside.

Cooking

Place a large pot over medium-high heat until hot. Add oil, swirling to coat sides. Add beef and brown on both sides. Drain off and discard any excess oil.

Pour braising sauce into pot and bring to a boil. Reduce heat, cover, and simmer, turning beef over occasionally, for 1½ to 2 hours or until beef is tender. Remove beef from pot, reserving braising sauce. Let beef cool, then cut into ½-inch cubes. Place beef cubes in a lightly greased 1-quart mold; set aside.

Sprinkle gelatin into ½ cup cold water; let set for 2 to 3 minutes.

Meanwhile, skim and discard fat from reserved braising sauce, then pour sauce through a fine strainer into a medium-size saucepan. Stir in softened gelatin. Bring braising sauce to a boil over medium-high heat, stirring until gelatin is dissolved. Reduce heat to medium; cook, uncovered, until sauce is reduced to approximately 2 cups. Refrigerate until slightly thickened, then pour sauce over beef in mold. Cover and refrigerate until set.

To serve, lower mold to its rim into warm water for a few seconds. Then cover it with a serving platter and invert to unmold, shaking gently to loosen. Lift off mold. Garnish with cilantro sprigs.

Tips

Substitute boneless lamb shank for the boneless beef chuck and garnish with mint leaves instead of cilantro.

TWICE-FRIED SHREDDED BEEF

Makes: 4 to 6 servings
Cooking time: 6 minutes

¾ pound beef sirloin or
flank steak

Marinade

2 tablespoons *each* dry
sherry and soy sauce
1 teaspoon *each* sugar and
cornstarch

1 small carrot
1 green bell pepper
2 stalks celery
1 small onion

Sauce

2 tablespoons rice vinegar
1 tablespoon soy sauce
2 teaspoons sesame oil
1 teaspoon sugar
½ teaspoon *each* chili oil
and cornstarch

Vegetable oil for deep-
frying

Preparation

Trim and discard excess fat from beef. Cut beef across the grain into 1½-inch matchstick pieces. Combine marinade ingredients in a medium-size bowl. Add beef; stir to coat. Set aside for 30 minutes.

Cut carrot, bell pepper, and celery into 1½-inch matchstick pieces. Thinly slice onion. Set vegetables aside separately.

Combine sauce ingredients in a small bowl and set aside.

Cooking

Set wok in a ring stand and add oil to a depth of 1½ to 2 inches. Place over high heat until oil reaches about 375°F. Add beef, half at a time, and deep-fry for 1 minute until browned, turning occasionally. Lift out and drain on paper towels; set aside. Cook remaining beef.

Remove all but 2 tablespoons oil from wok. Reheat oil over high heat until hot. Add carrot and onion; cook, stirring constantly, for 1 minute. Add bell pepper and celery; stir-fry for 1 more minute. Stir in sauce and beef. Cook and toss until well mixed.

Tips

There should be just enough sauce to coat ingredients.

It is easier to slice beef thinly if it is partially frozen.

Pictured on page 99

Peking

You'll find a wide variety of fresh Oriental vegetables in your local supermarket. Chinese markets carry an even greater supply of fresh as well as many preserved vegetables. For centuries the Chinese have used fermenting, pickling, salting, and drying to preserve surplus crops. While fresh produce is more readily available today, preserved vegetables are enjoyed for their unusual texture and flavor qualities. But you might want to try to grow your own vegetables. It's easy and fun. Try growing fresh snow peas (sugar peas), yard-long beans, or bok choy in your back yard. You can also grow snow peas, Chinese chives, or Chinese parsley (cilantro) in pots on a balcony.

One of the easiest grown Chinese vegetables is mung bean sprouts. In only 3 to 4 days you can harvest the crop. Here's how: First wash ½ cup of dried green mung beans, discarding any broken beans. Place in a one-quart jar with 2 cups of cold water. Cover with cheesecloth and secure the cloth tightly with string or a rubber band. The next day drain water, rinse the beans, drain again and let stand another night. Repeat this process 1 or 2 more days. When the white stems reach about 2½ to 3 inches in length, pick sprouts from the jar and rinse in a large bowl of water to remove the green husks. Drain well, place in a plastic bag, and use immediately or refrigerate up to 3 days.

"Fresh Chinese vegetables and herbs add authenticity to your cooking."

High in vitamins B and C, bok choy is easily grown in the garden. Plant seeds around March or April. This vegetable requires frequent, but light fertilizing. Crisp snow peas can be everybody's favorite. The pea pods are sweet and crunchy. They grow best in moist, non-acid soil with good drainage. For a spring crop, plant seeds in March or April. Plant seeds about 1-inch deep. Seeds germinate in 9-15 days. When seedlings are 3 inches tall, thin to 3 inches apart. Tie to a trellis.

For information on Chinese vegetable seeds, write to: Tsang and Ma, 1306 Old Country Road, Belmont, California 94002.

Martin Yan, The Chinese Chef

PEKING-STYLE EGGPLANT

Makes: 4 servings
Cooking time: 15 minutes

Sauce

- ⅓ cup chicken broth
- 2 tablespoons *each* soy sauce and rice vinegar
- 1 tablespoon dry sherry
- 2 teaspoons chili paste or ½ teaspoon chili oil

- 2 eggplants (about 1 pound each)

  Vegetable oil for deep-frying

- 3 cloves garlic, minced
- ½ teaspoon minced fresh ginger
- 3 green onions (including tops), cut diagonally into 2-inch pieces
- ¼ pound boneless lean pork, cut into matchstick pieces
- ½ teaspoon cornstarch mixed with 1 teaspoon water

  Hot cooked rice

Preparation

Combine sauce ingredients in a bowl and set aside. Peel eggplant if desired then cut into 2-inch matchstick.

Cooking

Set wok in a ring stand and add oil to a depth of 1½ to 2 inches. Place over high heat until oil reaches 375°F. Add eggplant, several pieces at a time, and deep-fry for about 2 minutes or until slightly limp. Lift out and drain on paper towels. Cook remaining eggplant.

Remove all but 1 tablespoon oil from wok. Reheat oil over high heat until hot. Add garlic and ginger; cook, stirring, until fragrant. Add green onions and pork; stir-fry for 3 minutes. Stir in sauce and eggplant; cook until heated through. Add cornstarch solution and cook, stirring, until sauce boils and thickens slightly. Serve over rice.

MANDARIN PANCAKES

Makes: About 16 pancakes
Cooking time: 30 minutes

2 cups all-purpose flour
¾ cup boiling water
2 tablespoons sesame oil

Preparation

Measure flour into a medium-size bowl. Mix in boiling water, stirring with chopsticks or a fork until dough is evenly moistened. On a lightly floured surface, knead dough for 5 to 6 minutes or until smooth and satiny. Cover with a damp cloth and let rest for 30 minutes.

On a lightly floured surface, roll dough into a 16-inch-long cylinder. Cut cylinder crosswise into 1-inch pieces. Shape each piece into a ball, then flatten slightly into a pancake. Pancakes should all be the same size. Brush top of each pancake with a light coating of sesame oil. Place one pancake on top of a second pancake, oil sides together. Using a rolling pin, roll the 2 pancakes together into a thin, 6-inch-diameter circle. Stack and roll remaining pancakes in the same way. Cover with a damp cloth and set aside.

Cooking

Place an ungreased wide frying pan with a nonstick finish over low heat. Add one double pancake and cook, turning once, for 2 minutes on each side or until both sides are lightly browned and bubbles appear on the surface. Remove from pan and separate into 2 pancakes while still hot. Stack cooked pancakes on a plate while cooking remaining double pancakes.

Tips

Pancakes can be prepared up to 1 day in advance and stored in a plastic bag in the refrigerator. Freeze for longer storage. To reheat, wrap pancakes in a clean dish cloth and steam in a bamboo steamer for 5 minutes. (You can also reheat pancakes in a microwave oven.)

Martin Yan, The Chinese Chef

SESAME BISCUITS

Makes: 18 biscuits
Cooking time: 15 minutes

2 tablespoons sesame seeds

Vegetable oil for deep-
frying

Dough

2 cups all-purpose flour
1 cup cake flour
2 teaspoons sugar
½ teaspoon salt
1⅓ cups boiling water

Preparation

In a wide frying pan, toast sesame seeds over medium-high heat for 5 minutes or until golden brown, shaking pan frequently. Remove and set aside.

Measure both kinds of flour, sugar, and salt in a bowl. Gradually add boiling water, stirring with chopsticks or a fork until dough is evenly moistened. On a lightly floured surface, knead dough for about 5 minutes or until smooth. Cover with a damp cloth and let rest for 30 minutes.

On a lightly floured surface, roll dough into a 12-inch long cylinder. Cut cylinder crosswise into 2-inch pieces. Roll each piece into a 4- by 8-inch rectangle. Sprinkle with 1 teaspoon toasted sesame seeds. Roll lightly with a rolling pin to incorporate sesame seeds into dough. Fold into thirds, then use a rolling pin to flatten slightly; set aside. Cover rectangles with a damp cloth while forming remaining dough.

Cooking

Set wok in a ring stand and add oil to a depth of 2 inches. Place over medium-high heat until oil reaches about 350°F. Add rectangles, two at a time, and deep-fry for 5 to 6 minutes or until golden brown, turning occasionally. Lift out and drain on paper towels. Keep rectangles warm in a 200°F oven while cooking remaining rectangles. Cut each rectangle into 3 pieces and serve hot.

Pictured on page 118

MANDARIN GLAZED APPLES

Makes: 16 to 20 apple wedges
Cooking time: 25 minutes

1 tablespoon fresh lemon
  juice
4 cups water
2 firm apples

Batter

⅔ cup all-purpose flour
¼ cup cornstarch
½ teaspoon baking powder
¾ cup water
3 teaspoons sesame oil

Syrup

¾ cup sugar
⅓ cup water

1 teaspoon vegetable oil

1 tablespoon sesame seeds

Vegetable oil for deep-
  frying

1 large bowl ice water

Preparation

In a large bowl, combine lemon juice and 4 cups water and set aside. Peel and core apples; cut each apple into 8 to 10 wedges. Drop apple wedges into lemon-water solution and set aside until ready to use.

Measure flour, cornstarch, and baking powder into a medium-size bowl. Gradually pour in ¾ cup water, whisking until smooth. Add 1½ teaspoons of the sesame oil; mix well. Set aside. Rub remaining 1 ½ teaspoons sesame oil on a serving platter; set aside.

Combine syrup ingredients in a heavy medium-size saucepan and set aside.

In a wide frying pan, toast sesame seeds over medium heat for about 5 minutes or until golden brown, shaking pan frequently. Remove and set aside.

Cooking

Set wok in a ring stand and pour oil to a depth of 2 inches. Place over high heat until oil reaches about 375°F. Drain apples well, then evenly coat apples with batter, letting excess drip off. Add apples, half at a time, and deep-fry for 3 to 4 minutes or until golden brown, turning constantly. Lift out and drain on paper towels.

Cook syrup over medium heat, stirring constantly, for 10 to 12 minutes or until mixture caramelizes (turns a light golden brown).

Form an assembly line of deep-fried apples, warm syrup, toasted sesame seeds, a large bowl of ice water, and the oiled serving platter. Dip each deep-fried apple wedge into warm syrup, turning to coat evenly. Coat with sesame seeds, dunk in ice water, then place on serving platter. Serve immediately.

Tips

Once the syrup begins to turn color, it will caramelize very rapidly—in less than a second. Cooking just a little too long can result in scorched

Martin Yan, The Chinese Chef

syrup. For best results with this recipe, we suggest that one person deep-fry the apples while the other person makes the syrup. Coat the hot apples the instant the syrup is ready and serve immediately.

Pictured on page 98

SWEET BEAN PASTE PUFF

Makes: 12 puffs
Cooking time: 12 minutes

Dough

2 tablespoons *each* sugar and lard
1 egg, lightly beaten
3 tablespoons water
1½ cups all-purpose flour
1¾ teaspoons baking powder

2 tablespoons sweet red bean paste
Vegetable oil for deep-frying

Preparation

Blend together sugar and lard in a small bowl. Add egg and water; mix until smooth.

In a separate bowl, measure flour and baking powder. Add sugar-lard mixture; blend well to make a smooth dough. Cover with a damp cloth and let rest for 15 minutes.

On a lightly floured surface, roll dough into a 12-inch-long cylinder. Cut crosswise into 1-inch pieces; shape each piece into a ball. To shape each dumpling, flatten one ball of dough with a rolling pin to make a 2½-inch circle. Place ½ teaspoon of bean paste in center of circle. Gather and pinch edges together at the top to seal securely. Roll carefully between your palms to form a round ball. Cover filled dumplings with a damp cloth while filling remaining dumplings.

Cooking

Set wok in a ring stand and add oil to a depth of 2 inches. Place over medium-high heat until oil reaches about 350°F. Add dumplings, a few at a time, and deep-fry for 3 to 4 minutes or until golden brown, turning occasionally. Lift out and drain on paper towels. Keep warm in a 200°F oven while cooking remaining dumplings. Serve immediately.

Pictured on page 99

Some 2000 years after the advent of wine, the delights of drinking tea *(cha)* were introduced in China during the Tang dynasty (A.D. 618–907). However, tea had been mentioned under a different name in Chinese literature as early as the Three Kingdoms (A.D. 220–265). But we mostly see its growth in popularity during the Sung (A.D. 960–1206) and the Mongol Yuan (A.D. 1271–1368) dynasties. An historical oddity is that Marco Polo never wrote about tea during his visit to China in 1275. So it is assumed that the Mongol leader Kublai Khan did not drink tea. Thus it took another 325 years for tea to reach Europe.

The preparation of tea underwent a number of changes over the centuries. The original method, as proposed by Lu Yu in his classic work *Cha Ching* (A.D. 780), was to boil tea leaves that had been pressed into cakes or bricks. The more Buddhist-oriented Sung beat powdered tea into hot water to create a froth. It wasn't until the early Ming dynasty (A.D. 1368–1644) that loose tea leaves were steeped in a pot or cup.

Tea grows abundantly all over China, and is generally categorized into three types: unfermented, fermented, and semi-fermented.

Unfermented tea, or green tea, is sun-dried and roasted immediately after picking. The refreshing, delicate flavor of green tea is most often enjoyed in such teas as Dragon Well (Lung Ching), Gunpowder, Lu An, Chrysanthemum (scented with Chrysanthemum blossoms), and the ever-popular Jasmine (also made with an Oolong base).

Fermented tea, or black tea, named for its black leaves (called red tea by Chinese for the red color the leaves impart), is full-bodied due to the fermentation of the leaves before roasting. Some of the black teas include Keemun, perhaps the most famous tea and the precursor to English Breakfast tea; Lapsang Souchong, a smoky-flavored tea; and Lychee (scented with the lychee fruit).

The semi-fermented teas capture the best characteristics of both the green and black teas. Oolong (Black Dragon) is most popular in China and abroad. Ti Kuan Yin (Iron Goddess of Mercy) from the Fujian province also falls into this category.

According to Chinese history, the use of the tea pot was not introduced until the Ming dynasty. Traditionally, the same pot is used over and over again for each type of tea. Pots are never washed, only rinsed, so as to retain the tea's flavor. Very old pots are said to have so much flavor that tea can be made in them without any leaves. The finest Chinese tea sets and pots are small, delicate, and exquisitely detailed works of art collected by many

To brew tea at home, here are some tips to follow: Tea should be brewed in earthenware, porcelain, or glass, and never in metal pots. First, rinse the pot with boiling water to heat it. Pour out the water and add one teaspoon of tea leaves per measuring cup of water. The water for the tea should be heated to just below boiling and poured over the tea leaves rather than adding the leaves to the hot water. Allow the tea to steep 3 to 5 minutes before serving. These same leaves can be used for a second pot of tea by simply adding more hot water.

Tea clears the palate, aids in digestion, soothes, uplifts, and refreshes. It is the one beverage you can't go wrong with when serving the flavors of China.

SHANGHAI

Shanghai, with its proximity to the far-reaching Yangtze River, relies heavily on the use of freshwater fish and shellfish in addition to its share of rice and fresh vegetables.

Martin Yan, The Chinese Chef

CLOCKWISE FROM TOP: *Sweet Date-filled Crepes* (page 160); *Classic Spring Rolls* (page 134); *chef Martin Yan inspecting vegetables; and Pineapple Honey Ham* (page 142).

> **"Shanghai's cuisine has extended its borders. Flavors and cooking methods reflect the influence of neighboring regions."**

The mighty Yangtze River, one of the world's longest rivers and the main artery through China's heartland, spawns the largest city in China—Shanghai.

The eastern region is traditionally known as the home of fish and rice. The temperate climate and fertile soil provide a multitude of crops, such as rice, tea, vegetables, and bamboo shoots. Trade along the Yangtze, and inland from the China Sea, provides other foodstuffs. The intricate network of rivers, canals, and lakes springing from the Yangtze provides an abundance of freshwater fish and shellfish, which naturally play a prominent role in the cuisine. Among the more well-known seafood delicacies are crab, prawns, and carp. But one can find just about any type of seafood dish prepared by the chefs of Shanghai, along with meat and poultry, served in rich, savory sauces.

Shanghai cuisine extends far beyond its boundaries and incorporates flavors and techniques from other areas. Fujian (Fukien) and Taiwan are well known for stews and soups, the broth being the trademark of their cuisine. Any leftover meats and bones are repeatedly boiled and filtered to produce the richest and most flavorful broth, used as a base in virtually all the dishes.

Suzhou (Soochow) is famous for its "red-cooking" technique where food is braised in a dark soy sauce to give it a rich reddish-brown hue (see "Red-Cooked Duck with Cabbage"). Sometimes rock sugar is used in red-cooking, producing a lighter, sweeter, silkier sauce unsurpassed anywhere.

Martin Yan, the Chinese Chef

East China is one of the few areas known for its fine wines and being the first to incorporate it as a seasoning into many dishes. It can be as obvious as "Drunken Chicken" or as subtle as "Braised Pork-Filled Cucumbers."

SUGGESTED MENUS

Shanghai Fish Soup
Red-Cooked Duck with Cabbage
Pineapple Honey Ham
Sweet Date-Filled Crepes

Braised Pork-Filled Cucumbers
Whole Sweet & Sour Fish
Bean Curd Family-Style
Pineapple Fried Rice

Tofu & Green Bean Salad
Hangchow Crispy Fish
Soy-Braised Beef
Eight Treasure Rice Pudding

Vegetarian Bean Curd Rolls
Mushrooms with Baby Bok Choy
Drunken Chicken
Yin Yang Rice

CLASSIC SPRING ROLLS

Makes: 8 to 10 rolls
Cooking time: 20 minutes

- 5 dried black mushrooms
- 1 teaspoon vegetable oil
- 2 eggs, lightly beaten

Filling

- 2 tablespoons vegetable oil
- ½ pound boneless lean pork, cut into matchstick pieces
- 2 green onions (including tops), cut into 1-inch slivers
- 1 cup *each* shredded cabbage or bok choy and bean sprouts
- ¼ cup *each* matchstick pieces bamboo shoots and chicken broth
- 2 tablespoons oyster sauce
- 2 teaspoons soy sauce
  Dash of white pepper
- 1½ teaspoons cornstarch mixed with 1 tablespoon water

- 8 to 10 spring roll or egg roll wrappers
- 1 egg white, lightly beaten
  Vegetable oil for deep-frying
  Plum Sauce (page 33) for dipping

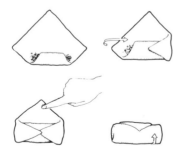

Preparation

Soak mushrooms in enough warm water to cover for 30 minutes; drain. Cut off and discard stems; thinly slice caps. Set aside.

Place a wide frying pan with a nonstick finish over medium-high heat until hot. Add 1 teaspoon oil, swirling to coat sides. Pour in eggs, tilting pan to coat bottom evenly. Cook just until eggs are set and feel dry on top. Remove from pan and let cool slightly. Cut into thin 1-inch-long strips and set aside.

Cooking

To make filling, place a wok or wide frying pan over high heat until hot. Add 2 tablespoons oil, swirling to coat sides. Add pork; stir-fry 2 minutes. Add mushrooms and filling ingredients except cornstarch solution; cook and toss for 2 more minutes. Add cornstarch solution and cook, stirring, until sauce boils and thickens. Remove from heat; toss in egg strips. Set aside to cool.

To fill each spring roll, mound about 2 heaping tablespoons of filling across one wrapper, keeping remaining wrappers covered to prevent drying (see illustration). Fold bottom corner over filling to cover, then fold over right and left corners. Roll over once to enclose filling. Brush sides and top of triangle with egg white. Fold over to seal. Cover filled spring rolls with a damp cloth while filling remaining wrappers.

Set wok in a ring stand and add oil to a depth of 2 inches. Place over medium-high heat until oil reaches about 360°F. Carefully add spring rolls, a few at a time, and deep-fry for 2 to 3 minutes or until golden brown, turning occasionally. Keep fried rolls warm in a 200°F oven while cooking remaining rolls.

Serve hot, with plum sauce for dipping.

Tips

In Chinese restaurants, spring rolls are often served with Worcestershire sauce.

Pictured on page 131

Martin Yan, the Chinese Chef

CHINESE CHICKEN SALAD

Makes: 4 to 6 servings
Cooking time: 10 minutes

Salad

4 cups shredded iceberg lettuce

1 cup shredded cooked chicken

½ cucumber, peeled, seeded, and cut into matchstick pieces

1 small carrot, cut into matchstick pieces

¼ cup bean sprouts

2 tablespoons shredded pickled ginger (optional)

½ cup sliced almonds

Dressing

3 tablespoons vegetable oil

1 teaspoon minced fresh ginger

1 clove garlic, minced

2 green onions (including tops), cut into 1-inch slivers

¼ cup rice vinegar

3 tablespoons soy sauce

1 tablespoon honey

1 teaspoon *each* sesame oil and chili oil

Dash of white pepper

Vegetable oil for deep-frying

1 ounce rice stick noodles, broken in half

Preparation

Combine salad ingredients in a large serving bowl and toss well. Cover and refrigerate.

Spread almonds in a shallow baking pan and roast in a 350°F oven for about 5 minutes, or until golden brown, shaking pan occasionally. Set aside.

Cooking

Place a small saucepan over medium-high heat until hot. Add 3 tablespoons oil, swirling to coat sides. Add ginger, garlic, and green onions; cook, stirring, for 1 minute. Add vinegar, soy sauce, honey, sesame oil, chili oil, and white pepper. Cook, stirring, until mixture comes to a boil. Remove from heat and set aside.

Set wok in a ring stand and add oil to a depth of 1½ to 2 inches. Place over high heat until oil reaches about 375°F. Add rice stick noodles and deep-fry for about 5 seconds or until they puff and expand. Turn over and cook other side. Lift out and drain on paper towels.

Drizzle dressing over salad; toss until well mixed. Just before serving, mix noodles and toasted almonds into salad. Serve at once, while noodles are still crisp.

Tips

Bean thread noodles are a good substitute for rice stick noodles. Both of these puff up instantly when dropped into hot oil, so cook them in small batches.

Pictured on page 150

Shanghai

TOFU & GREEN BEAN SALAD

Makes: 4 servings
Cooking time: 15 minutes

¼ cup dried shrimp

Dressing

1 tablespoon sesame seeds
1 tablespoon *each* sesame oil, soy sauce, and rice vinegar
1 teaspoon sugar
½ teaspoon *each* salt and chili oil or chili paste
Dash of white pepper

½ pound green beans
1 package (about 1 pound) firm tofu (bean curd), drained

Vegetable oil for deep-frying

Preparation

Soak shrimp in enough warm water to cover for 30 minutes; drain and set aside.

In a wide frying pan, toast sesame seeds over medium heat for about 5 minutes or until golden brown, shaking pan frequently. Combine sesame seeds and remaining dressing ingredients in a bowl; mix well. Set aside.

Remove ends and strings from green beans, then cut diagonally into 1½-inch pieces. Blanch green beans in boiling water for 2 to 3 minutes or until crisp-tender. Rinse under cold running water and drain. Set aside.

Cut tofu into 1- by 2-inch pieces. Drain on paper towels and set aside.

Cooking

Set wok in a ring stand and add oil to a depth of 1½ to 2 inches. Place over high heat until oil reaches 360° to 375°F. Add tofu, half at a time, and deep-fry for 5 to 6 minutes or until golden brown. Lift out and drain on paper towels. Cook remaining tofu.

Place shrimp, green beans, and tofu in a bowl. Pour dressing over and toss well. Cover and refrigerate. Serve cold.

Tips

To save time, you may use packaged deep-fried bean curd (available in Oriental markets) instead of frying your own.

Substitute pressed bean curd for the deep-fried bean curd. Follow same procedure.

Pictured on page 151

Martin Yan, the Chinese Chef

SHANGHAI FISH SOUP

Makes: 4 to 6 servings
Cooking time: 7 minutes

- 4 dried black mushrooms
- ½ pound white fish fillets (such as cod, sole, or red snapper)
- 1 tablespoon vegetable oil
- 1 tablespoon 1-inch slivers fresh ginger
- 2 tablespoons *each* red-in-snow and soy sauce
- 1 tablespoon dry sherry
- 1 teaspoon sugar
- 4 cups Basic Chicken Broth (page 106)
- ½ package (8 ounces) firm tofu (bean curd), drained and cut into ½-inch cubes
- 1 green onion (including top), cut diagonally into 1-inch pieces
- ½ teaspoon sesame oil

Preparation

Soak mushrooms in enough warm water to cover for 30 minutes; drain. Cut off and discard stems; thinly slice caps. Set aside.

Cut fish into 1- by 1½- pieces; set aside.

Cooking

Place wok over high heat until hot. Add oil, swirling to coat sides. Add ginger; cook, stirring, until fragrant. Add mushrooms, fish, and red-in-snow; stir-fry for 1 minute. Stir in soy sauce, sherry, sugar, broth, and tofu. Bring to a boil, stirring occasionally. Pour into a tureen and sprinkle with green onion and sesame oil. Serve hot.

Tips

Red-in-snow, available in cans in Chinese grocery stores, is a pungent, aromatic preserved vegetable. After opening, transfer to an airtight container and store in the refrigerator for several months. Red-in-snow is commonly used in casseroles, in soups, and in braised and stir-fried dishes.

Shanghai

APPLE BIRD

Using a small, sharp knife, cut a tiny V-shaped notch from the top of the apple. Continue making notches, a little larger each time than the previous cut (as shown). Continue until down to the lower front edge of the apple. Repeat procedure on the sides of the apple. Flare each section up and backward to simulate bird's head and wings.

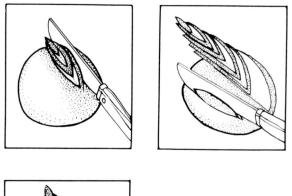

Martin Yan, the Chinese Chef

CUCUMBER FAN

Slice a cucumber in half lengthwise. Then cut one of the halves into 1 to 1½-inch-long pieces. Using a sharp knife, thinly slice cucumber section as shown, taking care to leave one edge intact. Fold up every other slice as shown, tucking in ends to secure. Flare out edges of cucumber and garnish edge of serving platter.

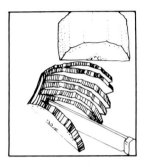  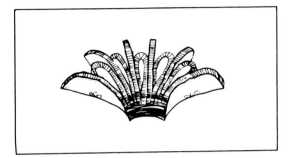

TOMATO FEATHER

Cut a firm tomato into wedges. Using a sharp knife, slice tomato skin and peel it back from one end, taking care to go no more than three-fourths of the way along the length of the wedge. Cut a deep, V-shaped wedge from the loosened skin. Stand feather upright along edge of plate for garnish.

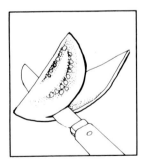  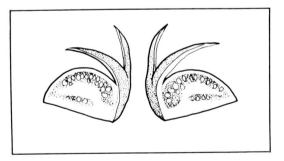

BRAISED PORK-FILLED CUCUMBERS

Makes: 4 servings
Cooking time: 16 minutes

Filling

- ⅔ pound ground lean pork or beef
- 1 tablespoon *each* soy sauce and dry sherry
- 2 teaspoons sesame oil
- 1 teaspoon *each* sugar and cornstarch

Sauce

- ⅓ cup chicken broth
- 2 tablespoons *each* soy sauce and dry sherry
- 1 teaspoon sugar

- 2 large cucumbers or fuzzy melons

  Cornstarch for coating

  Vegetable oil for deep-frying

- 2 teaspoons cornstarch mixed with 1 tablespoon water

Preparation

Combine filling ingredients in a bowl; mix well. Set aside for 30 minutes.

Combine sauce ingredients in a bowl and set aside.

Peel cucumbers if desired. Cut cucumbers crosswise into 1-inch thick sections; remove center of each section. Spoon about 1 level tablespoon of filling into each section. Lightly coat with cornstarch, shaking off excess. Set aside.

Cooking

Set wok in a ring stand and add oil to a depth of 1 ½ to 2 inches. Place over high heat until oil reaches 360° to 375°F. Add cucumber sections, a few at a time, and deep-fry for 2 minutes. Lift out and drain on paper towels. Cook remaining cucumber.

Place fried cucumber sections in a wide frying pan with a nonstick finish. Pour in sauce and bring to a boil. Reduce heat, cover, and simmer for 8 to 10 minutes. Add cornstarch solution and cook, stirring, until sauce boils and thickens. Arrange on a serving platter and serve hot.

Pictured on page 151

Martin Yan, the Chinese Chef

BEAN CURD FAMILY-STYLE

Makes: 6 servings
Cooking time: 12 minutes

Marinade

1 tablespoon *each* soy sauce
and dry sherry

1 teaspoon sesame oil

½ pound boneless lean pork
or beef flank steak, cut
into thin 1- by 2- by ¼-
inch slices

6 dried black mushrooms

Sauce

¾ cup chicken broth

¼ cup soy sauce

1 tablespoon *each* dry
sherry and sesame oil

1 package (about 1 pound)
firm tofu (bean curd),
drained

2 tablespoons vegetable oil

3 cloves garlic, minced

2 leeks (white part only), cut
diagonally into ½-inch
slices

1 can (8 ounces) sliced
bamboo shoots, drained

1 tablespoon cornstarch
mixed with 2 tablespoons
water

Hot cooked rice

Preparation

Combine marinade ingredients in a medium-size
bowl. Add pork; stir to coat. Set aside for 30
minutes.

Soak mushrooms in enough warm water to cover
for 30 minutes; drain. Cut off and discard stems;
thinly slice caps. Set aside.

Combine sauce ingredients in a small bowl and set
aside.

Cut tofu in half horizontally to make two 1-inch-
thick cakes. Cut each cake into quarters, then cut
again diagonally to form a total of 16 triangles. Drain
tofu triangles on paper towels and set aside.

Cooking

Place a wok or wide frying pan over high heat until
hot. Add oil, swirling to coat sides. Add garlic; cook,
stirring, until fragrant. Add pork and leeks; stir-fry for
2 to 3 minutes or until pork is lightly browned.

Add mushrooms, tofu, bamboo shoots, and sauce.
Reduce heat, and simmer, stirring occasionally, for
about 5 minutes or until leeks are crisp-tender. Add
cornstarch solution and cook, stirring, until sauce
boils and thickens. Transfer to a serving bowl and
serve over rice.

Tips

If you buy a 1-pound package of tofu containing
two 8-ounce cakes, simply cut each cake into 8
triangles.

This is a very popular, everyday dish.

PINEAPPLE HONEY HAM

Makes: 4 to 6 servings
Cooking time: 45 minutes

1½ pounds Smithfield or
    Virginia ham
1 can (8 ounces) sliced
    pineapple, packed in
    unsweetened pineapple
    juice
2 tablespoons dry sherry
1 tablespoon honey
½ teaspoon soy sauce
½ cup dried lotus seeds
2 tablespoons sugar
4 ounces rock sugar or ¼
    cup honey
1 tablespoon cornstarch
    mixed with 2 tablespoons
    water

Preparation

Cut ham into ½-inch-thick slices. Set aside.
Drain pineapple juice into a bowl and set pineapple slices aside. Stir sherry, honey, and soy sauce into pineapple juice.

Place lotus seeds in a medium-size saucepan and pour in enough water to cover. Bring to a boil over medium-high heat. Add sugar; stir until dissolved. Reduce heat, cover and simmer, stirring occasionally, for 35 to 40 minutes or until seeds are tender to bite. Drain and set aside.

Cooking

Place ham in a heatproof dish. Top with rock sugar and pineapple juice mixture. Set dish in a steamer or on a rack in a wok. Cover and steam over boiling water for 25 to 30 minutes or until rock sugar is completely melted. (If honey is used instead of rock sugar, simply steam ham for about 15 minutes or until heated through.) Remove ham from steamer and transfer to a serving platter.

Pour remaining juices from heatproof dish into a small saucepan and bring to a boil, stirring constantly. Add cornstarch solution and cook, stirring, until mixture boils and thickens.

Sprinkle lotus seeds over ham, then pour glaze over. Garnish with reserved pineapple slices.

Pictured on page 130

Martin Yan, the Chinese Chef

DRUNKEN CHICKEN

Makes: 4 servings
Cooking time: 40 minutes

Marinade

1 cup dry sherry or Shao
  Hsing wine
⅓ cup chicken broth
3 tablespoons soy sauce
1 teaspoon *each* minced
  fresh ginger and sugar
  Dash of white pepper

1 frying chicken (about 3
  pounds)
4 thin slices fresh ginger,
  each 1 by 2 inches
12 cups water

Preparation

Combine marinade ingredients in a bowl and set aside.

Cooking

Place chicken and ginger in a large pot. Pour water over chicken to cover. Bring to a boil, reduce heat, cover, and simmer for about 40 minutes or until meat near thighbone is no longer pink when slashed, turning chicken occasionally. Remove chicken and let cool to room temperature.

Remove and discard skin from chicken, if desired. Hand-shred chicken and place in a large bowl. Add marinade; stir to coat. Cover and refrigerate overnight. Serve cold.

Shanghai

ALMOND GAI DING

Makes: 4 servings
Cooking time: 13 minutes

Marinade

- 1 tablespoon soy sauce or oyster sauce
- 1 teaspoon *each* dry sherry, sesame oil, and cornstarch

- 1 whole chicken breast, boned and skinned, cut into ½-inch cubes
- ¼ pound medium-size raw shrimp, shelled and deveined
- ½ cup whole blanched almonds
- 2 tablespoons vegetable oil
- 1 clove garlic, minced
- 1 teaspoon minced fresh ginger
- 1 stalk celery, diced
- ½ cup 1-inch pieces asparagus, or ½ cup snow peas, ends and strings removed
- ½ carrot, diced
- 1 can (8 ounces) whole water chestnuts, drained and cut into quarters
- 1 green onion (including top), cut diagonally into ½-inch pieces
- ½ cup chicken broth
- 1 tablespoon dry sherry
- 1 teaspoon salt
- 1 teaspoon cornstarch mixed with 2 teaspoons water

  Hot cooked rice

Preparation

Combine marinade ingredients in a large bowl. Add chicken and shrimp; stir to coat. Set aside for 30 minutes.

Spread almonds in a shallow baking pan and roast in a 350°F oven for about 5 minutes or until golden brown, shaking pan occasionally. Set aside.

Cooking

Place a wok or wide frying pan over high heat until hot. Add oil, swirling to coat sides. Add garlic and ginger; cook, stirring, until fragrant. Add chicken and shrimp; cook and toss for about 3 minutes or until chicken is opaque and prawns are pink. Remove and set aside. Add celery, asparagus, carrot, water chestnuts, green onion, broth, sherry, and salt to wok; mix well. Cover and cook for 2 minutes. Return chicken and prawns to wok. Add cornstarch solution and cook, stirring, until sauce boils and thickens. Toss in roasted almonds and serve hot with rice.

Pictured on page 150

Martin Yan, the Chinese Chef

SHANGHAI SMOKED FISH

Makes: 4 servings
Cooking time: 40 minutes

Marinade

¼ cup soy sauce

2 tablespoons dry sherry

1 teaspoon minced fresh ginger

3 green onions (including tops), minced

1 pound red snapper fillets, cut into 3-inch squares

Vegetable oil for deep-frying

1 cup water

¼ cup packed brown sugar

1 teaspoon Chinese five-spice

½ head lettuce, shredded for garnish

Lemon wedges, for garnish

Preparation

Combine marinade ingredients in a bowl; mix well. Add fish; stir to coat. Cover and refrigerate for at least 4 to 6 hours or overnight, turning occasionally. Lift out fish and pat dry with paper towels. Reserve marinade.

Cooking

Set wok in a ring stand and add oil to a depth of 1½ to 2 inches. Place over medium-high heat until oil reaches about 360°F. Add fish, a few pieces at a time, and deep-fry for 4 to 5 minutes turning pieces to brown evenly. Lift out and drain on paper towels.

Bring reserved marinade, water, brown sugar and five-spice to a boil in a small saucepan, stirring constantly.

Place cooked fish in sauce, stirring to coat evenly. Lift out fish and drain well.

Reheat oil in wok over high heat until oil reaches about 375°F Add fish, a few pieces at a time, and deep-fry for 3 to 4 more minutes, turning occasionally. Lift out and drain on paper towels.

Arrange a bed of shredded lettuce on a serving platter. Place fish on top and garnish with lemon wedges.

Tips

This dish is not actually smoked—the combinations of seasonings give the fish a smoky look and flavor when deep-fried.

In China, fish is highly prized—not only as a delicacy for eating, but as a symbol for good luck and abundance. Although the written characters are different, the word for fish and the word for abundance are pronounced the same *yu*.

Many traditions have evolved centered around fish and luck. During northern Chinese winters, when fish were unobtainably trapped beneath frozen rivers, a carved wooden fish covered in savory sauce would be presented at the table. This would eliminate the possibility of having bad luck by tricking the gods.

In some parts of southern China, where families spend their entire lives on junks or sampans, the superstitions surrounding fish take a different form. Once cooked and presented on a plate, the fish is never turned over. Diners skillfully pick out the visible meat with chopsticks, then lift the bone from the plate to reach the meat on the underside, believing that if the fish is turned, their boats would capsize.

There are as many methods of preparing fish in China as there are myths and rituals surrounding fish. But steaming is the most common technique used to preserve the natural goodness.

In most cases the fish is cooked whole; the head is considered the best part and is coveted by gourmets. To offer the fish head to a guest or elderly person is considered an honor and a symbol of respect.

Steam-cooking is probably the simplest way to cook fish—all you need is boiling water. Pour about 2 inches of water into a wok or pot large enough to accomodate the fish you are steaming. Place a metal rack over the water, cover, and heat to boiling. Put the fish onto a deep heatproof plate and place on top of the rack. Cover wok and steam fish. Keep an eye on the water level to make sure the water doesn't boil away.

Steamed fish cools quickly, so try to steam the fish

on the same plate in which you will serve it. Scoring both sides of the fish will help the flavor of the other ingredients permeate the flesh, and will speed the cooking process. By poking the thickest part of the fish with a chopstick, you can test for doneness; the fish is ready when the flesh parts easily from the bone.

HANGCHOW CRISPY FISH

Makes: 4 servings
Cooking time: 15 minutes

- 1 whole fish (about 2 pounds) such as cod, red snapper, or sea bass, cleaned and scaled
- 1 teaspoon salt
  Cornstarch for coating
- 4 dried black mushrooms

Sauce

- ¾ cup chicken broth
- 2 tablespoons *each* soy sauce and dry sherry
- 1 fresh chili pepper, slivered (optional)
- 2½ teaspoons cornstarch mixed with 1½ tablespoons water
- 2 teaspoons *each* sugar, sesame oil, and chili paste

  Vegetable oil for deep-frying

- 2 cloves garlic, minced
- 1½ teaspoons 1-inch slivers fresh ginger
- ¼ pound boneless lean pork, cut into matchstick pieces
- 2 green onions (including tops), cut into 2-inch slivers
- ½ cup matchstick pieces bamboo shoots

Preparation

On each side of fish, make 3 or 4 diagonal slashes about 1-inch apart, cutting down to the bone each time. Rub fish with salt and cornstarch, shaking off excess. Set aside.

Soak mushrooms in enough warm water to cover for 30 minutes; drain. Cut off and discard stems; thinly slice caps. Set aside.

Combine sauce ingredients in a small bowl and set aside.

Cooking

Set wok in a ring stand and add oil to a depth of 2 inches. Place over medium-high heat until oil reaches about 360°F. Carefully lower fish into oil and deep-fry for 5 to 6 minutes, using a ladle to pour oil over fish to brown evenly. Carefully lift out with a large wire strainer or 2 spatulas and drain on paper towels. Transfer fish to a heatproof serving platter and keep warm in a 200°F oven.

Remove all but 2 tablespoons oil from wok. Reheat oil over high heat until hot. Add garlic and ginger; cook, stirring until fragrant. Add mushrooms, pork, green onions, and bamboo shoots; stir-fry for 3 to 4 minutes or until pork is browned. Add sauce and cook, stirring, until sauce boils and thickens slightly. Pour sauce over fish and serve hot.

Tips

Hangchow is a city near Shanghai, where this dish is often served as a regional specialty.

SEAFOOD WITH PAN-FRIED NOODLES

Makes: 4 to 6 servings
Cooking time: 20 minutes

  ½ pound *each* sea scallops
   and medium-size raw
   shrimp
  ¼ pound squid

Marinade

1½ teaspoons cornstarch
  1 teaspoon dry sherry
  ¼ teaspoon salt
   Dash of black pepper

Sauce

  1 cup chicken broth
  3 tablespoons oyster sauce
  2 tablespoons soy sauce
  1 tablespoon dry sherry
1½ tablespoons cornstarch
   mixed with 3 tablespoons
   water

  2 dried black mushrooms
  1 pound fresh noodles
 16 cups water
  ½ cup cold water
  1 tablespoon sesame oil
  3 tablespoons vegetable oil
  ¼ pound snow peas, ends
   and strings removed
  1 small onion, thinly sliced
  2 small carrots, cut into 2
   inch-slivers
  2 green onions (including
   tops), cut into 2-inch
   slivers

Preparation

Halve scallops horizontally; set aside. Shell shrimp, leaving tails attached. Split each shrimp along the back, cutting almost through to make shrimp lie flat; devein. Rinse and pat dry with paper towels. Set aside.

To clean squid, separate head and tentacles from body. Cut off tentacles just above eyes, then remove and discard hard beak at center of tentacles; rinse tentacles and set aside. Discard remainder of head. Pull out stiff pen from body. Slit body open and rinse throughly. Peel off speckled membrane and rinse again. Lightly score inside of body in a small crisscross pattern; cut body into 1½- by 2-inch pieces.

In a large bowl, combine marinade ingredients. Add squid pieces, scallops, and prawns; stir to coat. Set aside for 30 minutes.

Combine sauce ingredients in a bowl; set aside.

Soak mushrooms in enough warm water to cover for 30 minutes; drain. Cut off and discard stems; thinly slice caps. Set aside.

Cut noodles into 6-inch lengths. Bring 16 cups water to a boil in a large pot. Add noodles, stirring to separate strands. When water returns to a boil, add ½ cup cold water. Return to a boil again and cook, stirring occasionally, for 2 to 3 minutes or until noodles are tender to bite. Pour into a colander and rinse under cold running water; drain well. Toss noodles with sesame oil.

Martin Yan, the Chinese Chef

Cooking

Place a wide frying pan with a nonstick finish over medium heat until hot. Add 2 teaspoons of the oil, swirling to coat sides. Add half the noodles, spreading evenly over bottom of pan. Cook noodles for 3 to 4 minutes on each side or until golden brown on the bottom, swirling pan to prevent noodles from sticking; add more oil, if necessary. Place noodle "pancake" onto a large heatproof serving platter; keep warm in a 200°F oven while cooking remaining noodles.

Place a wok or wide frying pan over high heat until hot. Add 2 teaspoons of the oil, swirling to coat sides. Add scallops, shrimp, and squid; stir-fry for 3 minutes. Remove and set aside.

Add remaining 1 tablespoon vegetable oil to wok and place over high heat until hot. Add mushrooms, snow peas, onion, carrots, and green onions; stir-fry for 1 minute or until carrots are crisp-tender.

Return scallops, shrimp, and squid to wok. Add sauce; cook, stirring, until sauce boils and thickens slightly. To serve, spoon seafood-vegetable mixture evenly over noodle pancakes.

Tips
You can serve any meat and vegetable combination over noodle pancakes.

CLOCKWISE FROM RIGHT: Red-cooked Duck with Cabbage (page 154), Tofu & Green Bean Salad (page 136), Braised Pork-filled Cucumbers (page 140), and Whole Sweet & Sour Fish (page 152); Mushrooms with Baby Bok Choy (page 156); Almond Gail Ding (page 144); Chinese Chicken Salad (page 135); and Eight Treasure Rice Pudding (page 161).

Martin Yan, the Chinese Chef

Shanghai

WHOLE SWEET & SOUR FISH

Makes: 4 servings
Cooking time: 10 minutes

- 1 whole fish (2 to 3 pounds), such as sea bass or rock cod, cleaned and scaled
- 2 tablespoons dry sherry
- 1 teaspoon salt
- 4 dried black mushrooms
- 2 eggs, lightly beaten
  Cornstarch for coating

Sauce

- ½ cup water
- ¼ cup *each* rice vinegar and sugar
- 3 tablespoons ketchup
- 1 tablespoon *each* dry sherry and soy sauce
- ½ teaspoon chili oil
- 1½ tablespoons cornstarch mixed with 3 tablespoons water

  Vegetable oil for deep-frying

- 1 clove garlic, minced
- 1 tablespoon 1½-inch slivers fresh ginger
- 1 carrot, cut into 1½-inch slivers
- ½ green bell pepper, seeded and cut into 1½-inch slivers
- ½ cup 1½-inch slivers bamboo shoots
- 2 green onions (including tops), cut into 1½-inch slivers
- 2 tablespoons chicken broth

Preparation

On each side of fish, make 3 or 4 diagonal slashes about 1-inch apart, cutting down to the bone each time. Rub fish with sherry and salt; set aside.

Soak mushrooms in enough warm water to cover for 30 minutes; drain. Cut off and discard stems; thinly slice caps. Set aside.

Dip fish into eggs, then coat with cornstarch, shaking off excess. Let stand for 2 to 3 minutes.

Combine all sauce ingredients except cornstarch solution in a medium-size saucepan. Set aside.

Cooking

Set wok in a ring stand and add oil to a depth of 2½ inches. Place over high heat until oil reaches about 375°F. Carefully lower fish into oil and deep-fry for 5 to 6 minutes, using a ladle to pour oil over fish to brown evenly. Carefully lift out with a large wire strainer or 2 spatulas and drain on paper towels. Transfer to a heatproof serving platter and keep warm in a 200°F oven.

Remove all but 2 tablespoons oil from wok. Reheat oil high heat until hot. Add garlic and ginger; cook, stirring, until fragrant. Add carrot, bell pepper, bamboo shoots, green onions, and broth; stir-fry for about 1½ minutes or until vegetables are crisp-tender. Set aside.

Bring sauce to a boil over medium-high heat, stirring constantly. Add cornstarch solution and cook, stirring, until sauce boils and thickens. Remove from heat; add stir-fried vegetables and stir to coat. Pour vegetables and sauce over fish; serve hot.

Pictured on page 151

Martin Yan, the Chinese Chef

SOY-BRAISED BEEF

Makes: 4 to 6 servings
Cooking time: 2¼ hours

1½ pounds boneless beef
  chuck, cut into 1-inch
  cubes
1 tablespoon soy sauce
8 to 10 cloud ears
1 small Chinese white
  radish (about 1 pound)

Braising Sauce

2 cups water
¼ cup dry sherry or Shao
  Hsing wine
3 tablespoons dark soy
  sauce
2 tablespoons packed dark
  brown sugar
4 thin slices fresh ginger,
  each 1 by 2 inches
1 whole star anise
2 green onions (including
  tops), cut in half
1 piece dried tangerine peel

1 to 2 tablespoons vegetable
  oil
1½ tablespoons cornstarch
  mixed with 3 tablespoons
  water

Hot cooked rice or
  noodles

Preparation

In a large bowl, combine beef and soy sauce; stir to coat. Set aside for 30 minutes.

Soak cloud ears in enough warm water to cover for 30 minutes; drain.

Peel radish and cut in half horizontally, then cut each half diagonally into ½-inch-thick slices. Set aside.

Combine braising sauce ingredients in a medium-size bowl and set aside.

Cooking

Place a large pot over medium-high heat until hot. Add oil, swirling to coat sides. Add beef; cook, stirring constantly, until browned. Stir in braising sauce and bring to a boil. Reduce heat, cover, and simmer for 1½ hours, stirring occasionally. Add cloud ears and radish. Cover and continue to simmer for about 30 more minutes or until beef is tender. Drain beef and reserve sauce. Transfer beef to a heatproof serving platter and keep warm in a 200°F oven.

Pour sauce through a fine strainer into a saucepan and bring to a boil. Add cornstarch solution and cook, stirring, until sauce boils and thickens. Pour sauce over beef cubes and serve hot over rice or noodles.

Tips

Pre-cut boneless beef chuck, often referred to as stew meat, can be purchased in your supermarket.

RED-COOKED DUCK WITH CABBAGE

Makes: 6 to 8 servings
Cooking time: 2 hours

- 1 duckling (4 to 5 pounds), cleaned

Marinade

- 2 tablespoons dark soy sauce
- 1 tablespoon dry sherry

Sauce

- 3 cups Basic Chicken Broth (page 106)
- ¼ cup *each* dry sherry or Shao Hsing wine and dark soy sauce
- 2 green onions (including tops), cut in half
- 4 thin slices fresh ginger, *each* 1 by 2 inches
- 3 cloves garlic, minced
- 2 whole star anise
- 1 small cinnamon stick
- 4 teaspoons sugar
- 1 teaspoon sesame oil

- 1 small Chinese (napa) cabbage (about ½ pound), leaves separated
- 2 tablespoons vegetable oil
- 2½ teaspoons cornstarch mixed with 1½ tablespoons water

Preparation

Cut off and discard excess neck skin from duck. Remove and discard fat from around body cavity; cut off tail. Prick duck all over with a bamboo skewer. Combine marinade ingredients in a large bowl. Add duck; rub duck inside and out with marinade. Cover and refrigerate for 1 hour, turning occasionally. Drain duck and set aside.

Combine sauce ingredients in a large pot and set aside.

Blanch cabbage leaves in boiling water for 5 to 6 minutes or until tender to bite. Rinse under cold running water; drain well. Cut into bite-size pieces and set aside.

Cooking

Place a wok or wide frying pan over medium-high heat until hot. Add oil, swirling to coat sides. Add duck and cook for about 2 minutes on all sides or until evenly browned.

Bring sauce to a boil. Add duck; reduce heat, cover, and simmer for about 1¾ hours or until duck is tender and skin is a rich brown, turning duck occasionally.

Carefully lift duck from pot, reserving sauce. Debone duck, if desired, then cut into serving-size pieces. Place duck pieces on a heatproof serving platter, arranging them in the shape of a whole duck. Keep warm in a 200°F oven.

Skim and discard fat from braising sauce. Combine ⅔ cup of the braising sauce with cornstarch solution in a small saucepan. Cook over medium-high heat, stirring, until sauce boils and thickens slightly.

Arrange cabbage around duck. Pour sauce over duck and serve hot.

Pictured on page 151

Martin Yan, the Chinese Chef

VEGETARIAN BEAN CURD ROLL

Makes: 6 rolls
Cooking time: 50 minutes

Filling

1 cup glutinous rice
6 dried black mushrooms
1 tablespoon vegetable oil
1 clove garlic, minced
½ small carrot, cut into 1-inch slivers
3 asparagus tips, cut diagonally into ½ inch pieces, or ¼ cup frozen peas, thawed
¼ cup 1 inch slivers bamboo shoots
¼ cup canned gingko nuts, drained (optional)
2 pitted dates, coarsely chopped
2 green onions (including tops), cut into 2 inch slivers
2 tablespoons soy sauce
1 tablespoon hoisin sauce
2 teaspoons *each* dry sherry and sesame oil

6 dried bean curd sheets
1 tablespoon flour mixed with 1 tablespoon water
6 tablespoons vegetable oil

Preparation

Soak rice in enough warm water to cover for 30 minutes; drain.

Line the inside of a steamer with a damp cheesecloth. Place rice on cheesecloth. Cover and steam over boiling water for 30 minutes. Lift out and set aside.

Soak mushrooms in enough warm water to cover for 30 minutes; drain. Cut off and discard stems; thinly slice caps. Set aside.

Cooking

Place a wok or a wide frying pan over medium-high heat until hot. Add oil, swirling to coat sides. Add garlic; cook, stirring, until fragrant. Add carrot and asparagus; cook and toss for about 2 minutes or until vegetables are crisp-tender. Add mushrooms, bamboo shoots, gingko nuts, dates, onions, soy sauce, hoisin sauce, sherry, and sesame oil. Stir-fry for 2 minutes. Add rice; cook and toss, until well mixed. Transfer to a bowl and set aside.

Soak bean curd sheets in enough warm water to cover for 3 to 4 minutes or until softened; drain. To fill each bean curd sheet, spread about 2 heaping tablespoons of filling across one sheet, keep remaining sheets covered to prevent drying. (Refer to illustration for wrapping Classic Spring Rolls, page 134.) Fold bottom corner over filling to cover, then fold over right and left corners. Roll over once to enclose filling. Brush sides and top of triangle with flour paste. Fold over to seal. Filled bean curd rolls should resemble a thick oblong package. Cover filled bean curd sheets with a damp cloth while filling remaining sheets.

Place a wide frying pan with a non-stick finish over medium heat. Add 2 tablespoons oil, swirling to coat sides. Add bean curd rolls, two at a time, and cook for 2 minutes on each side or until golden

(continued on next page)

(continued from previous page)

brown. Transfer to a heatproof dish and keep warm in a 200°F oven while cooking remaining rolls. To serve, cut each bean curd roll into thirds; serve hot.

Tips
When soaked for over 15 minutes, bean curd sheets may be fragile and difficult to handle.

MUSHROOMS WITH BABY BOK CHOY

Makes: 4 servings
Cooking time: 18 minutes

12 medium dried black mushrooms

Sauce
¾ cup chicken broth
1 tablespoon *each* soy sauce, oyster sauce, and dry sherry
1 teaspoon cornstarch mixed in 2 teaspoons water

1 can (8 ounces) button mushrooms, drained
1 ounce Smithfield or Virginia ham, diced

1 pound baby bok choy
8 cups water
1 teaspoon oil
¼ teaspoon salt

Preparation

Soak mushrooms in enough warm water to cover for 30 minutes; drain. Cut off and discard stems; leave caps whole. Set aside.

Combine sauce ingredients, black mushrooms, and button mushrooms in a medium-size saucepan.

Cut each bunch of bok choy in half lengthwise and set aside.

Cooking

Bring water, oil, and salt to a boil in a large pot. Blanch bok choy for about 5 minutes or until tender to bite. Rinse under cold running water and drain well. Arrange bok choy attractively on an oval serving platter. Set aside.

Bring sauce and mushrooms to a boil; reduce heat, cover, and simmer for 10 minutes.

Spoon mushrooms and sauce over bok choy. Sprinkle with ham. Serve hot.

Pictured on page 150

Martin Yan, the Chinese Chef

STEAMED WHITE RICE

Makes: About 3 cups
Cooking time: 25 minutes

1 cup long grain rice
1½ cups water

Cooking

Place rice in a 2-quart pan. Rinse rice briefly under cold running water to remove excess starch and any foreign particles; drain. Pour in 1½ cups water. Bring rice to a boil over medium-high heat. Boil, uncovered, for about 10 minutes or until water evaporates and crater-like holes appear. Reduce heat, cover, and simmer for about 15 minutes or until rice is soft and tender. Remove from heat and let set for 8-10 minutes before serving. Fluff and serve hot.

PINEAPPLE FRIED RICE

Makes: 4 servings
Cooking time: 10 minutes

4 teaspoons vegetable oil

1 egg, lightly beaten

2 strips lean bacon, coarsely chopped

½ medium onion, finely chopped

½ cup small cooked shrimp

¼ cup diced ham

4 green onions (including tops), finely chopped

4 cups cooked long-grain rice

2 tablespoons *each* chicken broth and soy sauce

2 teaspoons sesame oil

½ teaspoon salt

2 slices canned pineapple, drained and diced

¼ cup chopped unsalted roasted cashews or almonds (optional)

Cooking

Place a wide frying pan with a nonstick finish over medium-high heat until hot. Add 1 teaspoon of the vegetable oil, swirling to coat sides. Pour in egg; tilting pan to coat bottom evenly. Cook just until egg is set and feels dry on top. Remove egg from pan and let cool slightly, then cut into thin 1-inch long strips. Set aside.

Place a wok or wide frying pan over high heat until hot. Add remaining 3 teaspoons vegetable oil, swirling to coat sides. Add bacon and onion; cook, stirring constantly, for about 1 minute or until onion is limp and translucent. Add shrimp, ham, green onions, and rice; stir-fry until well blended. Stir in broth, soy sauce, sesame oil, and salt. Cook and toss for 2 more minutes or until rice is heated through. Remove from heat. Add pineapple, egg strips, and nuts; toss to mix. Place in a serving bowl.

Tips

Cooled rice is easier to cook with than hot. I personally prefer using fresh-cooked rice, which is moist and flavorful.

Fried rice is one of the most popular one-dish meals in many parts of China.

YIN YANG RICE

Makes: 6 servings
Cooking time: 10 minutes

- 1 tablespoon vegetable oil
- 1 egg, lightly beaten
- 4 cups cooked rice
- 1 teaspoon sesame oil
- ½ teaspoon salt

Yin Sauce

- 1 tablespoon vegetable oil
- ¼ pound small cooked shrimp
- ⅓ cup evaporated milk
- ¼ cup *each* chicken broth and frozen peas, thawed
- ½ teaspoon each sesame oil, salt, and sugar
- 1 teaspoon cornstarch mixed with 2 teaspoons water

Yang Sauce

- 1½ tablespoons vegetable oil
- 1 green onion (including top), finely chopped
- ¼ pound ground lean beef
- 1 cup coarsely chopped tomatoes
- 3 tablespoons ketchup
- 1 teaspoon dry sherry
- ½ teaspoon sugar
- 1 teaspoon cornstarch mixed with 2 teaspoons water

Cooking

Place a wok or wide frying pan over medium-high heat until hot. Add oil, swirling to coat sides. Pour in egg, tilting wok to coat bottom evenly. Cook, turning constantly until egg is set. Add rice, tossing, to evenly distribute egg. Add sesame oil and salt; mix well. Transfer to a heatproof serving platter; cover and keep warm in a 200°F oven.

To make yin sauce, place a saucepan over medium-high heat until hot. Add oil, swirling to coat sides. Add shrimp; cook for 1 minute. Reduce heat to medium then stir in remaining yin ingredients. Cook, stirring, until sauce boils and thickens slightly. Set aside and keep warm.

To make yang sauce, place clean wok over medium-high heat until hot. Add oil, swirling to coat sides. Add green onion and beef; stir-fry for about 1½ minutes or until beef is lightly browned. Stir in tomatoes, ketchup, sherry, and sugar; cook for 1 minute. Add cornstarch solution and cook, stirring, until sauce boils and thickens slightly.

To serve, spoon yin sauce over one half of the rice and yang sauce over the other half.

Martin Yan, the Chinese Chef

For thousands of years the Chinese have followed the Taoist philosophy of cosmic equilibrium—the balanced harmony of all things. One of the simplest forms of this philosophy is the idea of two opposing forces in balance—*yin* and *yang*. Yin represents the feminine, cooler, moister, and weaker forces, while yang comprises the masculine, warmer, drier, and stronger forces.

Chinese cooks follow this philosophy by selecting a combination of foods that balance yin and yang, to keep the body in equilibrium and maintain good health. Foods are cooked, then classified according to how they affect the body; the actual temperature of the food is not taken into consideration. "Hot" or yang foods such as chili peppers, ginger, fried foods, and red meats are thought to increase the pulse rate and perspiration. This removes excess moisture from the body. "Cold" or yin foods such as winter melons, asparagus, and crab meat cleanse, soothe, and moisturize the body.

Many Chinese believe that when the lips crack or the nose bleeds, the body is too dry and the system has too much yang force. Yin foods should be eaten to bring the body back into balance. When the weather is humid, people tend to be weak and tired and the body retains too much moisture. Yang foods are then eaten to bring the yin forces back into equilibrium. By following this philosophy, the Chinese have been serving nutritionally balanced meals for centuries.

When planning your menu, strive for a balance of color, texture, flavor, and cooking techniques. This too is part of the traditional Chinese concept of contrast and balance.

"Yin and Yang...
**two opposing forces
in balance."**

SWEET DATE-FILLED CREPES

Makes: 24 to 27 pieces
Cooking time: 30 minutes

Crepes

1 cup all-purpose flour
1 egg, lightly beaten
1 cup water
2 tablespoons butter

Date Paste

½ pound pitted dates
¼ cup water
1 teaspoon sugar (optional)

About 5 teaspoons
vegetable oil
2 tablespoons chopped
unsalted roasted peanuts

Preparation

Measure flour into a medium-size bowl. Using a fork, blend egg into flour until mixture is crumbly. Add 1 cup water, a few tablespoons at a time, stirring well after each addition. Add melted butter and beat until batter becomes smooth and silky. Let stand for 15 minutes.

In a food processor or blender, whirl dates, ¼ cup water, and sugar into a smooth paste. Transfer to a bowl and set aside.

Cooking

Place a 10-inch frying pan with a nonstick finish over medium-high heat until hot. Add 1 teaspoon of the oil and wipe with a dry paper towel. Pour ¼ cup batter into center of pan. Immediately tilt pan in all directions so batter spreads to form a thin 6- to 7-inch crepe. Cook crepe for about 45 seconds or until it is completely set and surface feels dry when lightly touched. Loosen edges with a spatula, turn over, and cook for 30 more seconds. Remove and stack crepes on a platter while cooking remaining crepes.

Smooth 1 heaping tablespoon of date paste across the center of each crepe, leaving about 1 inch exposed on each end. Sprinkle paste with peanuts. Fold exposed ends over filling; then fold each side over, completely enclosing date paste. Filled crepes should resemble an oblong package.

Place a wide frying pan with a nonstick finish over medium-high heat until hot. Add 1 teaspoon of the oil, swirling to coat. Cook filled crepes, a few at a time, for 1½ to 2 minutes on each side or until golden brown, swirling pan over heat to brown evenly. Add more oil as needed. Cut each crepe into thirds. Serve hot.

Pictured on page 131

Martin Yan, the Chinese Chef

EIGHT TREASURE RICE PUDDING

Makes: 4 to 6 servings
Cooking time: 1 ½ hours

2 cups glutinous rice,
   rinsed and drained

2 cups water

¼ cup solid vegetable
   shortening or lard, melted

2 tablespoons sugar

Eight Treasure Garnish

2 tablespoons sliced roasted
   almonds

6 candied red dates

8 to 10 canned whole lotus
   seeds (optional)

4 *each* candied red and
   green cherries

2 tablespoons raisins

3 or 4 candied kumquats
   (optional)

⅔ cup sweet red bean paste

Syrup

¾ cup water

⅓ cup honey

4 teaspoons Triple Sec or
   Grand Marnier

2 teaspoons cornstarch
   mixed with 1 tablespoon
   water

Preparation

In a medium-size saucepan, bring rice and water to a boil over medium-high heat. Boil, uncovered, for about 10 minutes or until water evaporates and crater-like holes appear. Reduce heat, cover, and simmer for 25 to 30 minutes. Fluff rice, then stir in melted shortening and sugar and set aside.

Meanwhile, generously grease a 1-quart glass bowl. Arrange almonds, dates, lotus seeds, red and green cherries, raisins, and kumquats attractively over bottom of bowl. Carefully spread half the cooked rice over fruit-nut decoration; avoid disturbing decoration. Press rice down lightly. Spoon bean paste over rice, forming a smooth, even layer. Cover with remaining rice, spreading evenly. Cover bowl with a small damp cloth.

Cooking

Place covered bowl in a steamer or on a rack in a wok. Cover with a lid and steam over gently boiling water for 1 hour, replenishing water when necessary.

Meanwhile, place syrup over medium heat, swirling pan occasionally. Continue to cook until syrup is reduced to ½ cup, stirring constantly. Keep warm. Just before serving, add Triple Sec and mix well.

Cover mold with a serving platter and invert, gently shaking to unmold. Pour hot syrup over pudding. Serve hot.

Tips

This is a classic dessert served at formal banquet dinners. Angelica may be used in place of candied cherries.

Pictured on page 150

NOUVELLE CHINESE

Nouvelle Chinese cuisine is the epitome of "East meets West" because it blends new flavors with centuries-old practices. It is becoming an integral part of contemporary Chinese cooking.

Martin Yan, the Chinese Chef

CLOCKWISE FROM TOP RIGHT: *Fresh Ginger Ice Cream; Lop Cheong Baked Clams (page 166); Pineapple-Lemon Chicken (page 170); chef Martin Yan preparing Braised Orange Duck (page 173); and Beef with Chinese Steak Sauce (page 172).*

Nouvelle Chinese

When people move, so do lifestyles. In almost every country we find a multitude of communities, and we find their ways of life, particularly their cuisines, becoming part of the native culture. The Chinese have long been active emigrants, and their cuisine has been very much a part of that.

We now see adaptations of Chinese cuisine all over the world. Consider the Chinese noodle (developed during the Han dynasty, 206 B.C.-A.D. 220, shortly after the technique of flour-milling was imported from India) that we all know and love as spaghetti. But, what have the Chinese borrowed from the West?

Did you know that Chinese parsley, or cilantro as it is sometimes called, is not from China, but originated in the Middle East, along with grapes, pomegranates, walnuts, squash, and that all-important ingredient in Chinese cooking, sesame seed? All came to China by way of the Silk Road. And the sweet and crispy snow pea that we use in so many stir-fried dishes actually comes from Europe. In China, they refer to it as the Holland pea.

"Be like the great chefs of China... learn to experiment with new flavors."

Although rice has been a staple in China since 4000 B.C., the Chinese have more recently taken to the potato, as well as cooking with such Western seasonings as ketchup, Worcestershire sauce, and curries from India and Indonesia. Don't be surprised if you see Tabasco (Western-style chili sauce) on the restaurant table. All of these have become an integral part of the Chinese cuisine. This blending of ideas in NOUVELLE CHINESE, as you will see in the following recipes, allows unlimited creativity in the kitchen.

You'll find that Chinese cuisine clamors to be experimented with—and that is the oldest tradition of all.

Martin Yan, the Chinese Chef

CRISPY SHRIMP ROLLS

Makes: 14 to 16 rolls
Cooking time: 20 minutes

Paste

1 egg, lightly beaten
1 pound medium-size raw
shrimp, shelled and
deveined
4 teaspoons cornstarch
2 teaspoons sesame oil
½ teaspoon salt
Dash of black pepper

14 to 16 slices white
sandwich bread
Cilantro (Chinese parsley)
leaves
2 ounces Smithfield
or Virginia ham, cut
into 2½-inch-long
matchstick pieces

Vegetable oil, for
deep-frying

Preparation

In a food processor or blender, combine half the beaten egg with remaining paste ingredients. Whirl to a smooth paste and set aside. Reserve remaining beaten egg.

Cut off and discard bread crusts, then flatten slices with a rolling pin to a thickness of ¼ inch. Spread paste evenly over three-fourths of each bread slice, leaving one side (about one-fourth of the surface) uncovered. Sprinkle a few cilantro leaves on top of paste, then lay 2 pieces of ham along center of each slice of bread. Brush uncovered surface with reserved beaten egg. Starting from paste side, roll each slice into a cylinder, pressing lightly to seal.

Cooking

Set wok in a ring stand and add oil to a depth of 1½ to 2 inches. Place over medium-high heat until oil reaches 350° to 360°F. Add shrimp rolls, a few at a time, and deep-fry for 3 to 4 minutes or until rolls turn golden brown and float to the surface. Lift out and drain on paper towels. Transfer rolls to a heatproof dish and keep warm in a 200°F oven while cooking remaining rolls.

Cut rolls into 1-inch pieces and serve hot.

Tips:

Serve these rolls as an appetizer with Homemade Sweet & Sour Sauce (page 33) or Hot Mustard Sauce (page 32) mixed with soy sauce.

LOP CHEONG BAKED CLAMS

Makes: 10 appetizers
Cooking time: 20 minutes

4 dried black mushrooms

10 medium-size live hard-shell clams

½ pound medium-size raw shrimp, shelled, deveined and coarsely chopped

1 Chinese sausage (2 ounces), coarsely chopped

6 to 8 water chestnuts, coarsely chopped

3 green onions (white parts only), finely chopped

1 egg, lightly beaten

1 clove garlic, minced

1 tablespoon dry sherry

1 tablespoon finely chopped cilantro (Chinese parsley)

2 teaspoons minced fresh ginger

2 teaspoons cornstarch

½ teaspoon salt

Dash of black pepper

½ cup fine dry bread crumbs

Rock salt

Preparation

Soak mushrooms in enough warm water to cover for 30 minutes; drain. Cut off and discard stems; coarsely chop caps. Set aside.

Scrub clams well with a stiff brush, then soak in enough salted water to cover for 30 minutes to draw out sand; drain.

Cooking

Place clams in a heatproof dish. Set dish in a steamer or on a rack in a wok. Cover and steam over boiling water for 7 to 8 minutes or until shells open. Let clams cool, then remove from shells; reserve shells. Coarsely chop clams and set aside.

Place mushrooms, clams, shrimp, sausage, water chestnuts, green onions, egg, garlic, sherry, cilantro, ginger, cornstarch, salt, and pepper in a medium-size bowl. Mix well.

Mound clam mixture on one side of each shell, pressing down on top of mound to flatten and smooth. Evenly sprinkle bread crumbs over stuffed clams, lightly pressing down on surface to coat well.

Arrange clams, filled side up, in an ovenproof serving dish lined with rock salt. Bake in a 400°F oven for 10 to 12 minutes or until golden brown. Serve hot.

Tips:

The amount of clam mixture placed in the shell depends on the shell size.

Mussels may be substituted for the clams.

Pictured on page 163

Martin Yan, the Chinese Chef

CITRUS-SPICED SPARERIBS

Makes: 4 servings
Cooking time: 24 minutes

- 1½ to 2 pounds pork spareribs

Marinade

- 3 tablespoons *each* soy sauce and dry sherry
- ¼ teaspoon *each* Chinese five-spice and salt

- 1 egg, lightly beaten
- ⅓ cup all-purpose flour

  Vegetable oil, for deep-frying

Braising Sauce

- 2 teaspoons vegetable oil
- ½ teaspoon minced fresh ginger
- 2 shallots, minced
- ⅓ cup fresh orange juice
- ¼ cup *each* frozen tangerine juice concentrate and fresh lemon juice
- 3 tablespoons packed brown sugar
- 2 tablespoons fresh lime juice
- 2 teaspoons grated lemon peel
- 1 teaspoon cornstarch mixed with 2 teaspoons water

  Orange wedges, for garnish

Preparation

Trim and discard excess fat from spareribs, then cut ribs apart between bones. Combine marinade ingredients in a large bowl. Add spareribs, stirring to coat all sides. Cover and refrigerate for at least 4 hours or overnight.

Drain ribs briefly. Dip ribs in egg, then coat evenly with flour, shaking off excess. Set on a plate and let stand for 10 minutes.

Cooking

Set wok in a ring stand and add oil to a depth of 1½ to 2 inches. Place over medium-high heat until oil reaches about 350°F. Add spareribs, 4 or 5 pieces at a time, and deep-fry, turning occasionally, for about 8 minutes or until golden brown. Lift out and drain on paper towels. Cook remaining ribs.

Meanwhile, place a wide frying pan over medium-high heat until hot. Add oil, swirling to coat sides. Add ginger and shallots; cook, stirring, until fragrant. Add remaining braising sauce ingredients and cook, stirring, until sauce boils and thickens slightly. Reduce heat and add ribs to pan. Simmer, uncovered, over medium-low heat, turning ribs occasionally, for about 5 minutes or until ribs are well coated. Garnish with orange wedges and serve hot.

Tips:

For handy bite-size hors d'oeuvres, ask your butcher to cut across the ribs into 2-inch strips.

STIR-FRIED MILK OVER A CLOUD

Makes: 4 servings
Cooking time: 10 minutes

Milk Mixture

⅔ cup evaporated milk

½ cup milk

6 egg whites, lightly beaten

1 tablespoon cornstarch

1 teaspoon sesame oil

½ teaspoon salt

Dash of white pepper

Vegetable oil, for deep-frying

1 ounce rice stick or bean thread noodles, broken in half

¼ pound cooked crabmeat, shredded

2 ounces Smithfield or Virginia ham, cut into matchstick pieces

Cilantro (Chinese parsley) sprigs, for garnish

Preparation

In a medium-size bowl, whisk together milk mixture ingredients until foamy; set aside.

Cooking

Set wok in a ring stand and add oil to a depth of 1½ to 2 inches. Place over high heat until oil reaches 360° to 375°F. Add rice stick noodles and deep-fry for about 5 seconds or until they puff and expand. Turn over and cook other side. Lift out and drain on paper towels. Place noodles on a serving platter, pressing down on noodles to flatten slightly; set aside.

Place a wide frying pan with a nonstick finish over medium-high heat until hot. Add 2 teaspoons oil, swirling to coat sides. Pour in half the milk mixture. Cook, stirring, for 2 to 3 minutes or until soft curds form. Transfer to a bowl, cover, and keep warm while cooking remaining milk mixture.

To serve, spoon all the curd mixture over noodles. Arrange crabmeat in center of mixture and surround with ham. Garnish with cilantro. Serve immediately.

Tips:

Since rice stick and bean thread noodles puff up instantly in hot oil, fry only a small handful at a time.

Martin Yan, the Chinese Chef

CHEESE-FILLED GOLDEN CRAB

Makes: 4 servings
Cooking time: 10 minutes

1 Dungeness crab (about
1 ¾ pounds), cooked,
cracked, and cleaned,
with back shell left whole

Filling

5 dried black mushrooms

2 eggs, lightly beaten

½ cup grated Jack cheese

2 tablespoons *each*
chopped Smithfield or
Virginia ham and minced
shallots

1 tablespoon cornstarch
mixed with 2 tablespoons
water

1 tablespoon *each* minced
cilantro (Chinese parsley)
and brandy

2 teaspoons sesame oil

½ teaspoon sugar

¼ teaspoon salt

⅛ teaspoon white pepper

2 tablespoons Panko (bread
crumbs)

Vegetable oil, for
deep-frying

Preparation

Wash back shell; pat dry and set aside. Shred crabmeat and set aside.

Soak mushrooms in enough warm water to cover for 30 minutes; drain. Cut off and discard stems; thinly slice caps.

In a medium-size bowl, combine crabmeat and mushrooms with remaining filling ingredients; mix well.

Mound filling into reserved back shell, pressing firmly to make a smooth, solid mound.

Cooking

Place stuffed crab shell on a heatproof dish. Set dish in a steamer or on a rack in wok. Cover and steam over boiling water for 8 minutes. Carefully lift out crab. Sprinkle stuffed side evenly with panko.

Set a clean wok in a ring stand and add oil to a depth of 1½ to 2 inches. Place over high heat until oil reaches about 375°F. Lower crab, crumb side up, into oil. Ladle hot oil over crab to evenly brown. Cook for about 1 minute or until crumb topping is golden brown. Lift out and drain, crumb side up, on paper towels. Serve hot.

Tips:

Prepare filling just before steaming; otherwise mixture will become watery.

Panko, Japanese-style bread crumbs, are white, flaky and coarser than regular bread crumbs. Panko gives deep-fried foods a light, crispy coating.

PINEAPPLE-LEMON CHICKEN

Makes: 4 servings
Cooking time: 8 minutes

2 whole chicken breasts,
   split, skinned and boned
¼ teaspoon salt
   Dash of black pepper
1 tablespoon dry sherry

Lemon Sauce

2 slices canned pineapple,
   cut into quarters
¼ cup *each* fresh lemon
   juice and water
3 tablespoons packed
   brown sugar
2 tablespoons rice vinegar
1 tablespoon butter
2 teaspoons vegetable oil
1¼ teaspoons cornstarch
1 teaspoon *each* grated
   lemon peel and minced
   fresh ginger

1 cup Panko (bread crumbs)
¼ cup sesame seeds
1 egg, lightly beaten

   Vegetable oil, for
   deep-frying

   Pineapple slices, for
   garnish

Preparation

Pound each chicken breast half to flatten. Place chicken in a bowl and add salt, pepper, and sherry; stir to coat. Set aside for 30 minutes.

To make lemon sauce, whirl pineapple slices in a blender until smooth. Then combine with remaining sauce ingredients in a small saucepan; set aside.

In a shallow bowl, combine Panko and sesame seeds. Dip chicken into egg, then roll in Panko-sesame seed mixture, shaking off excess. Set aside for 5 minutes.

Cooking

Set wok in a ring stand and add oil to a depth of 2 inches. Place over medium-high heat until oil reaches 350° to 360°F. Add chicken, 2 pieces at a time, and deep-fry for 3 to 4 minutes or until golden brown and meat is no longer pink when slashed, turning occasionally. Lift out and drain on paper towels. Place on a heatproof dish and keep warm in a 200°F oven while deep-frying remaining chicken.

Meanwhile, cook sauce over medium-high heat, stirring, until sauce boils and thickens slightly.

Cut chicken into strips and arrange on a serving platter. Pour sauce over chicken and garnish edge of platter with pineapple slices. Serve hot.

Tips:

For a crispier crust, fry the chicken a second time before serving.

Pictured on page 162

Martin Yan, the Chinese Chef

GRILLED GINGER STEAK

Makes: 4 servings
Cooking time: About 6 minutes

Marinade

⅓ cup soy sauce

¼ cup dry sherry

2 cloves garlic, minced

1½ tablespoons minced fresh
     ginger

1 tablespoon vegetable oil

¾ teaspoon ground, toasted
     Szechuan peppercorns

1½ to 2 pounds T-bone or
     New York steaks, cut
     1-inch thick

Preparation

Combine marinade ingredients, reserving
¼ teaspoon of the ground peppercorns; mix well.
Place steaks in a shallow baking pan, then pour
marinade over steaks. Cover and refrigerate for
2 to 4 hours.

Cooking

Lift steaks from marinade and drain briefly.
Place on a grill 3 to 4 inches above a solid bed of low-
glowing coals. (Or place 2 to 3 inches below heat
on a rack in a broiler pan.) Cook, turning once, for
3 minutes on each side, for medium-rare or until
done to your liking.

Cut steaks into thick slices and arrange on a warm
platter. Sprinkle with reserved ¼ teaspoon ground
peppercorns to serve.

Tips:

You can thicken remaining marinade and use as
a sauce to pour over steaks.

Nouvelle Chinese

BEEF WITH CHINESE STEAK SAUCE

Makes: 4 servings
Cooking time: 10 minutes

1 pound beef sirloin or
flank steak

Marinade

1 tablespoon *each* soy
sauce, water, and dry
sherry
2 teaspoons sesame oil
1 teaspoon cornstarch

Sauce

2 tablespoons hot ketchup
1 tablespoon *each* hoisin
sauce and steak sauce
2 teaspoons *each*
Worcestershire sauce and
packed brown sugar
½ teaspoon Tabasco sauce

Vegetable oil, for
deep-frying

2 ounces bean thread
noodles, broken in half
1 green onion (including
top), finely chopped

Preparation

Trim and discard fat from beef. Cut beef across the grain into 3- by 2- by ¼-inch slices. Combine marinade ingredients in a bowl and add beef; stir to coat. Cover and refrigerate for 2 hours.

Combine sauce ingredients in a bowl; mix well and set aside.

Cooking

Set wok in a ring stand and add oil to a depth of 1½ to 2 inches. Place over high heat until oil reaches about 375°F. Add half the bean thread noodles and deep-fry for about 5 seconds or until they puff and expand. Turn over and cook other side. Lift out and drain on paper towels. Cook remaining noodles. Place noodles on a serving platter, pressing down on noodles to flatten slightly; set aside.

Remove all but 2 tablespoons oil from wok. Add beef, 6 or 7 pieces at a time, and cook for about 1 to 1½ minutes on each side or until done to your liking. As beef is cooked, transfer it to a bowl; set aside while cooking remaining beef.

Return all beef to wok and place over medium heat. Pour sauce over beef and cook, stirring to coat well, for 2 minutes.

Spoon beef over noodles and sprinkle with green onion. Serve hot.

Tips:

Adjust the amount of Tabasco sauce to taste.
For a spicier flavor, substitute sweet bean sauce for hoisin sauce.

Pictured on page 163

BRAISED ORANGE DUCK

Makes: 6 to 8 servings
Cooking time: 2 hours

- 1 duckling (4 to 5 pounds), cleaned
- ¾ teaspoon salt
- ½ teaspoon black pepper
- 2 tablespoons rice vinegar
- 1 tablespoon *each* dark soy sauce and honey

Braising Sauce

- 2½ cups Basic Chicken Broth (page 106)
- 1½ cups fresh orange juice
- 3 tablespoons grated orange peel
- 2 tablespoons *each* lemon juice, soy sauce, and packed brown sugar
- 1 piece dried tangerine peel

- 3 tablespoons vegetable oil
- 4 shallots, sliced
- 2 tablespoons *each* brandy and Triple Sec
- ½ teaspoon cornstarch mixed with 1 teaspoon water

Preparation

Cut off and discard excess neck skin from duck. Remove and discard fat from around body cavity; cut off tail. Prick duck all over with a bamboo skewer.

Place duck in a large pot with enough water to cover and bring to a boil. Carefully lift out duck and place in a colander; rinse under cold running water. Drain and pat dry, inside and out. Sprinkle duck inside and out with salt and pepper.

Combine vinegar, soy sauce and honey; mix well. Brush mixture on duck to coat evenly. Cover and refrigerate for 6 hours.

Combine braising sauce ingredients in a bowl; mix well and set aside.

Cooking

Place duck, breast side up, on a rack over a foil-lined baking pan. Roast in a 425°F oven for 30 minutes or until skin is lightly browned.

Place a heavy pot (large enough to hold duck) over high heat until hot. Add oil, swirling to coat sides. Add shallots; cook, stirring, until limp and translucent. Stir in brandy and then braising sauce. Lower duck into pot. Ladle some of the sauce into duck body cavity and over duck. Bring to a boil, then reduce heat. Cover and simmer, turning occasionally, for 1¼ hours or until duck is tender and skin is a rich brown.

Lift out duck, drain and place on a serving platter. Slowly bring remaining sauce to a boil. Stir in Triple Sec and cornstarch solution. Cook, stirring, until sauce boils and thickens slightly. Pour sauce over duck and serve.

Pictured on page 162

POTATO PORK PANCAKES

Makes: 4 servings
Cooking time: 36 minutes

  4 dried black mushrooms
  2 eggs, lightly beaten
  ¼ cup cornstarch
  2 teaspoons sesame oil
  ½ teaspoon salt
  Dash of white pepper

Sauce

  ¾ cup chicken broth
  1 green onion (including top), minced
  ½ teaspoon minced fresh ginger
  1 tablespoon cornstarch mixed with 2 tablespoons water

  About 2 tablespoons vegetable oil
  1 clove garlic, minced
  ¼ teaspoon minced fresh ginger
  ¼ pound ground lean pork
  2 medium russet potatoes, peeled and grated
  2 green onions (including tops), minced
  ¼ cup chopped water chestnuts

Preparation

Soak mushrooms in enough warm water to cover for 30 minutes; drain. Cut off and discard stems; coarsely chop caps. Set aside.

In a large bowl, beat eggs with cornstarch, sesame oil, salt, and white pepper; set aside.

In a small saucepan, combine sauce ingredients and set aside.

Cooking

Place a wide frying pan with a non-stick finish over medium-high heat until hot. Add 2 teaspoons oil, swirling to coat sides. Add garlic, ginger, and pork; stir-fry for 1½ to 2 minutes or until pork is browned. Remove, drain, and set aside to cool. Combine cooled pork with egg mixture, mushrooms, potato, green onions, and water chestnuts; mix well.

Place clean frying pan over medium-high heat until hot. Add about 1 teaspoon oil, swirling to coat sides. Pour in ½ cup of potato mixture, tilting pan to form a 5-inch pancake. Cook for about 4 minutes on each side or until golden brown. As pancakes are made, transfer them to a heatproof dish and place in a 200°F oven to keep warm.

Meanwhile, cook sauce over medium-high heat, stirring until sauce boils and thickens. Place pancakes on a serving platter. Pour sauce over and serve hot.

STEAMED HONEY-PLUM PEARS

Makes: 4 servings
Cooking time: 25 minutes

4 firm ripe pears (such as
Anjou or Bosc)

Filling

2 tablespoons honey
1 tablespoon plum sauce
1 whole star anise, broken
into 4 pieces
Dash of ground cinnamon

Sauce

2 tablespoons *each* honey
and plum sauce
1 tablespoon plum wine
1 teaspoon chopped pickled
ginger
¼ teaspoon cornstarch
mixed with ½ teaspoon
water

Preparation

Peel pears, leaving stems attached. Cut off 1 inch
from top of each pear; reserve tops. Carefully core
pears.

Combine filling ingredients until well blended.
Spoon enough filling into each cavity to fill pears,
allowing one piece of star anise for each pear. Cover
pears with reserved tops and place in a heatproof
dish.

Cooking

Set dish in a steamer or on a rack in a wok. Cover
and steam over boiling water for about 25 minutes or
until pears are tender.

Meanwhile, combine sauce ingredients in a small
saucepan. Cook over medium heat, stirring, until
sauce boils and thickens slightly; keep warm.

Remove star anise pieces from filling, then place
steamed pears in individual serving bowls. Spoon
sauce over pears and serve hot.

Nouvelle Chinese

CONVERSION TABLE FOR METRIC MEASUREMENTS

All recipes in this book use the imperial measurements. This chart will give you a guideline for converting the weight and volume measurements to metric equivalents. By converting a few recipes you should get the hang of it — it is not too hard. Besides, a slight variation in the weight will not significantly change the recipe.

IMPERIAL	METRIC	IMPERIAL	METRIC
Volume		**Weight**	
1/2 teaspoon	2 ml	1/2 ounce	14 grams
1 teaspoon	5 ml	1 ounce	28 grams
1/2 tablespoon	7 ml	2 ounces	56 grams
1 tablespoon	15 ml	4 ounces (1/4 pound)	112 grams
1/4 cup	60 ml	6 ounces	168 grams
1/3 cup	80 ml	8 ounces (1/2 pound)	225 grams
1/2 cup	125 ml	10 ounces	280 grams
3/4 cup	200 ml	12 ounces	340 grams
1 cup	250 ml	16 ounces (1 pound)	450 grams
1 1/4 cups	310 ml	1 1/2 pounds	675 grams
1 1/2 cups	370 ml	2 pounds	900 grams
1 3/4 cups	430 ml	4 pounds	1800 grams
2 cups	500 ml		
4 cups	1 liter		
6 cups	1 1/2 liters		
Measurements		**Temperature**	
1/4 inch	0.5 cm	Fahrenheit	Celsius
1/2 inch	1 cm	275	140
1 inch	2.5 cm	300	150
2 inches	5 cm	325	160
3 inches	7.5 cm	350	180
4 inches	10 cm	375	190
		400	200

OTHER HELPFUL CONVERSION FACTORS

Ingredient	Imperial	Metric (Approx.)
Rice/Flour/Sugar	1 cup	220 grams
Sugar	1 teaspoon	10 grams (5 ml)
Cornstarch/Salt	1 teaspoon	5 grams (5 ml)
Cornstarch/Salt	1 tablespoon	15 grams (15 ml)

INDEX

YAN CAN COOK
Wishes To Thank The Support
Of Our Partners

If it doesn't cireles,
it's not Cireulon.

Maker of Oriental sauces since 1888.

We bring good things to life.

Aroma therapy for the kitchen.

Freshest ideas in produce
and specialty foods.

Yan Can Cook, Inc.,
P.O. Box 4755, Foster City, CA 94404
E-Mail: yccook@aol.com
Website:http//www.yancancook.com